MODERN
HIGH-SECURITY
LOCKS

To Delores

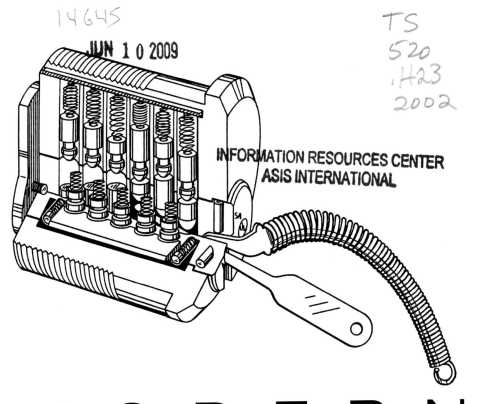

MODERN
HIGH-SECURITY
LOCKS

HOW TO OPEN THEM

Steven Hampton

Paladin Press · Boulder, Colorado

Also by Steven Hampton:

Advanced Lock Picking Secrets
Affordable Security
Patent Secrets (w/Craig Herrington)
Secrets of Lock Picking
Security Systems Simplified

Modern High-Security Locks:
How to Open Them
by Steven Hampton

Copyright © 2002 by Steven Hampton
ISBN 10: 1-58160-295-2
ISBN 13: 978-1-58160-295-1
Printed in the United States of America

Published by Paladin Press, a division of
Paladin Enterprises, Inc.
Gunbarrel Tech Center
7077 Winchester Circle
Boulder, Colorado 80301 USA
+1.303.443.7250

Direct inquiries and/or orders to the above address.

PALADIN, PALADIN PRESS, and the "horse head" design
are trademarks belonging to Paladin Enterprises and
registered in United States Patent and Trademark Office.

Ballpoint ink drawings by Steven Hampton.
Drawings based on original lock and key art courtesy of:
ABUS, Abloy, ASSA, ASSA/Abloy Group, Chicago Lock, Fort Locks,
Hirsch Electronics, Ilco Unican, KABA, Key Devices, Medeco, Ruko,
Securitron, TuBar Security, and Van Lock

Visit our Web site at www.paladin-press.com

Contents

Warning

The author, publisher, and distributors of this book in no way endorse or condone any potentially illegal activity or act and disclaim any liability for the use or misuse of the information contained herein. This book is *for information purposes only*.

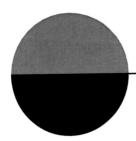

Preface

When *Secrets of Lock Picking* first appeared in 1987, I felt somewhat concerned about the possibility of someone using my information for illegal purposes. But then I realized most criminals do not have the patience to pick open a lock or the skills needed to make the tools. Since the publication of *Secrets of Lock Picking*, the national burglary rate (as well as crime in general) has dropped per capita. Not because of the book, of course, but in spite of it.

This suggests that information alone is not the precursor to crime—it is poverty and poverty mentality that spark crime. In any society, crime is a political disease, not just an emotional one. Good government should not alienate its citizens with unfair taxes, regulations, and favoritism. And though our democracy has grown complex and is by no means perfect, so may be our own judgment should we suddenly find ourselves immersed in poverty—imagined or real.

But blaming our poverty on the system does not justify committing a theft. Ultimately, we are responsible for our own destinies. So we must use this kind of information wisely and rise above that first, sudden impulse to steal, because doing so would cause another's loss and suffering, accompanied by anger and perhaps even a sad loss of faith in man.

We all know empathetically what is right, and deep in our bones we know what feels wrong. As enlightened beings we can carefully weigh our choices and see what we are up against in the War on Crime. You do not want to enter that battlefield. You will lose. This information is for reference only—or to help someone in need. Knowledge is a double-edged sword that cuts both enemy and holder; only the hand of compassion can safely wield it.

Real wealth is found in the heart.

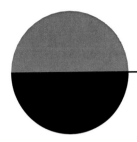

Introduction

I decided to write this follow-up to *Secrets of Lock Picking* at the request of many of my readers. Herein I have evaluated various new locks on the market and designed and made tools to test their security. In so doing, I have collected a series of some of the more popular pick-resistant locks and set out see which ones held up to their claims. This catalog is not intended to devalue the security of these locks, but rather to instill in the manufacturer the awareness that security is a never-ending battle and none of them can rest on their laurels.

It is also in the best interest of the locksmith to know how these locks are rated in pick resistance. Furthermore, my evaluation would be meaningless if I did not show the reader how they are picked. After all, the security of a lock is not rated just by knowing how to pick it, but by the time it takes to pick it.

AN EVOLUTIONARY BEGINNING—
THE PIN TUMBLER LOCK

The modern pin tumbler lock was invented in the mid-1820s by Linus Yale, Sr.[1] All good, present-day mechanical locks are based on his invention: a cylinder that contains a series of spring-loaded pins (or wafers in subsequent inventions) that restrict its rotation. This type of security has worked well for almost two centuries, even though its beginnings can be traced back 5,000 years.[2] But with the new wave of electronic locks and multi-functional mechanisms, being locked out today may have a whole new meaning. And though this is good news for the world of security, when keys are lost or the circuit fails, the locksmith is faced with a daunting challenge—to open the expensive lock without destroying it. Also, in most cases, destroying the lock could make matters worst.

The ability to pick locks open is considered a magical feat, the reason being that the pin tumbler lock is supposedly invincible. But any lock with an access port can be picked if you have the skill and enough time.

With new lock designs being developed every year someplace on the planet, it becomes ever more difficult to keep up with all the different systems. When I first started working with locks as a pimply-faced teenager in the 1960s, I had no idea how far this would go. James Bond-type palm-reading locks, voice recognition, not to mention space-age retina scanners, were just fiction then. Now they are a reality. These are real, functioning systems not yet available to the general public. Some are being used in selected industrial and government facilities. The U.S. Army is perfecting this new field, called "biometrics." This complex system uses a video camera to scan people's eyes, the shapes of their ears, their voices, and even their movement. This information is then fed into microprocessing and is used to allow access to buildings and military bases. Some systems can even detect a particular person's body odor and are programmed to open a lock when that scent is detected. So how does one go about opening the locks in an emergency?

Today, there seem to be nine different classifications of keyed pin tumbler locks alone. Most of them are hybrids of past successful systems. The evolutionary path of hybrid locks has led to finely machined mechanisms that fit together with such precision that greater sensitivity and skill are required to pick them. As such, I have classified and arranged the various mechanisms into chapters by order of complexity.

Generally speaking, the more complex a lock, the more secure it is. However complex the lock gets, though, it must be durable, dependable, and user-friendly. It has to be tough enough to endure physical attack, but it can't be machined too tight or it will jam up with just a breath of dust. It must be simple and easy to lock and unlock with its key or the customer will not pay the higher price for it.

It is this delicate balance between security and utility that allows the lock picker to open this new generation of locks.

In this volume, I can only cover some of the more popular high-security locks—most of which evolved from the lowly pin tumbler cylinder lock. The real challenging systems are not yet available for study to the majority of us, though we might see them occasionally. I will try to keep the technical jargon to a minimum, when possible, and fill you in on the latest systems and how you might possibly open them.

Please note that most of the following lock illustrations are redrawn from patent copy, so there are a few subtle differences between some of the figures and the actual lock or key. Many times once an invention is patented, modifications are made to the finished product. Naturally these changes would have to be small or the patent would not apply to the end product. I have drawn in these various modifications to depict the actual lock where possible. In Chapter 3, the differences were great enough to warrant drawing the patent version (Figure 3J) and the actual lock (Figure 3I). In all other cases, any differences between lock and key and their illustrations are very minor and do not affect how the lock functions or how it is picked.

I have personally picked nearly all of these locks. Those that I had a good deal of trouble with and could not open, I gave the highest pick-resistance rating and included in the text anyway so that you may take a crack at them if you wish. Hopefully my advice will help you. At the very least, you'll discover which ones are best suited for your customer's application.

PICK-RESISTANCE RATING SYSTEM

We have devised a security rating scale of **1** to **15** in half-steps, based on the difficulty in picking the lock and the time it takes to open it. For example, the tiny, single-lever, riveted-case Master padlock model #44 (the first lock I ever picked and no longer in production) or a simple jewelry box lock rates at **1** for ease of picking, as only two simple actions are involved within a time frame of two seconds: sticking in the pick key and turning it.

An example of a pick-resistance **2**-rated lock would be a double-lever warded, laminated Master padlock model #22D, as this requires a little searching for the two levers hidden within the laminate wards and intermittent tugging of the shackle to pop it open.[3] Average pick time, about 15 seconds.

A lock with a pick resistance rating of **3** would be a five-wafer cylinder desk lock such as a National or Welsh, either of which can be picked in about 30 seconds.

Standard five-pin tumbler cylinder locks such as a Quikset or Weslock, the tight keyway of a wafer tumbler Hurd lock, and the Chicago double-wafer desk lock are pick resistance rated at **4** and are usually picked within 45 seconds.

A five-pin tumbler Yale lock (no spools or mushroom pins[4]) that has its pins keyed to near-level shear plane is rated at **5**. This is because the slant and tightness of the keyway is the major security issue, not the number of tumblers and varied shear lines. A Schlage double-wafer knob lock would also fall into this category. Pick time: under 60 seconds.

With a rating of **6** the security starts to get pretty good. A few prime examples would be a Corbin, Russwin, or Yale spool and/or mushroom pin tumbler lock. Or a Dexter, Weiser, or Ilco with a high degree of varied pin tumbler shear lines. I can usually pick one of these in between 90 and 120 seconds on a good day with a White Crane Feather Touch tension wrench and a thin (.018″ to .022″) standard diamond pick.

Ratings of **6.5** and higher will be given to the locks we are about to encounter—so find a comfortable chair, we're off to explore the best security available on the market today. By the way, a **7.5** is typical of automotive side-bar locks. A pick-resistance value of **15** would be considered unpickable. These locks would include such mechanisms as digitally controlled, high-security safe locks or card readers, for instance. This is the range of the new high-security locks today.

A FEW WORDS OF CAUTION

As with my previous books, I must warn the reader that the information contained within these pages is for eyes only. If you are using this information for illegal reasons, you will eventually get caught. There is only one professional cat burglar that I know of who has retired out of prison—and he is a 78-year-old pauper.

Forensic science has evolved to a point where crime just does not pay. For example, in the near future, DNA from a few skin cells could convict you. Since everyone constantly sheds skin in the hundreds of thousands of cells per hour, getting away with a high-stakes theft will be very rare indeed (unless the thief is wearing a sealed body suit, which would make the job unbearable). If a reader is prosecuted, Paladin Press and I will naturally side with the authorities, because though I find stories and movies about cat burglars interesting and entertaining, I personally have no respect for thieves.

Also, with the popular (and often disturbing) uses of various types of miniature video cameras and recorders today, you can't get away with anything anyway. Along with silent helicopters and satellite cameras, this is one more infringement on our personal freedom. On a side note, though it reduces crime, I find this reduction of our privacy an expensive price to pay. It is a tough call to determine which is more important, but Big Brother seems to have decided for us.

On the brighter side, if you learn the techniques in this book, your skills could help someone who is locked out of his or her home, business, or car. Just be certain that the one you are helping is the proper owner of that property. Ask for I.D. or a neighbor's OK. To open a lock in such a dubious situation would be practicing "idiot" compassion. But in all other cases, picking locks can be a satisfying and often rewarding hobby. There is a sense of power and pride as well. Remember to use visualization while picking.

Visualization Techniques

Visualization within this context implies a deliberate, conscious effort to "see" the inner workings of a lock within the mind's eye. Below is an old, secret, Tibetan Buddhist tantric visualization exercise. Here I have modified it for the reader to use for lock picking, but the essence of the technique is the same.

Step One

First, remove your shoes and put on comfortable, loose-fitting clothing such as sweats or shorts and a T-shirt if it is warm. Remove all tight jewelry, such as rings (you may keep your wedding band on if you wish), chokers, and bracelets. Remove eyeglasses (contacts are OK) as well. Remove as much metal from your person as possible.

Step Two

You may begin the technique by sitting upright in a comfortable chair with your hands in you lap and feet flat on the floor. Don't slouch or recline, as this will make it too easy for you to fall asleep. Keep your spine straight, but not stiff. The chair should have a comfortable headrest. Most newer car seats are good examples of an ideal chair, as comfort and alertness are important. Also, a good office chair will work very nicely. Or you may choose to practice the traditional method by sitting cross-legged on the floor on a four- to six-inch cushion. The point is not to let your head tilt back. Your neck should align comfortably with your spine. Tuck your chin in slightly. Your tailbone should be tilted slightly forward, but with your hips at a comfortable angle. If your hips are properly aligned forward, you will not need a headrest, as your straight spine and neck will comfortably balance your head, which is in the ideal position.

Step Three

The room should be quiet, with no music, and dimly lit or dark, with no candles or incense. Sit down and settle in for a few minutes.

Step Four

Now close your eyes. Breathe in deeply, but not forcefully, through your nose. Feel the life flow into your lungs, filling you with vitality and lightness. Do not hold the breath, but let it flow out naturally, dissolving into the room, filling the space. Do this for several breaths.

Step Five

Now breathe normally, relaxing any tight muscles in your body. This can be accomplished by just focusing attention on various parts of the body and letting go of those parts. Just abandon them. If you feel an itch, abandon it—it will go away by itself.

Start by relaxing the jaw muscles. Let them go, but don't gape your mouth completely open. Just crack your lips and let the breath come and go gently, naturally through both lips and nose.

Relax your facial muscles. Relax the tiny muscles around the eyes and forehead. Then let go of the neck muscles. Now relax the shoulders, let them drop comfortably back and down, gently drawing the shoulder blades closer together. Relax the shoulder blades. Relax the rib cage and chest with each out-breath. Let go of the upper arms. Relax the fore-arms, letting the fingers open naturally in the lap.

Let the stomach muscles go—feel the warmth in the belly. Let go of the thigh muscles and calves. Then feel the feet dissolve away as well. Let the whole body dissolve away. Just sit there for a few minutes and enjoy this pleasant, tingling warmth vibrating through the whole being.

Step Six

Now, with eyes still closed, gently bring attention to the forehead—the focal point between the eyes—about where the eyebrows join. With eyelids closed, focus the eyes there without straining. Just let the breath come and go without strain, without clinging. After a few minutes or less, a series of images will flash into view. In this darkness these images will even take on the shapes of faces. This is natural; don't be alarmed or concerned with them. Gently concentrate on forming a simple, round white ball between the eyes and keep focused on it. Here, size doesn't matter much, but for reference, imagine the size of a softball at arm's length away. Don't let it become anything but a smooth, white ball.

The ball will want to rise. But gently bring it back down into view. If you let it rise above your head, you might lose consciousness and fall asleep. Gently hold it level between the eyes with the mind, casually viewing it as if you were an isolated, detached observer. You have no investment in this ball, but you will not let it stray from your empty gaze, either.

Practice this technique for 20 minutes. You may set a timer if you wish, as long as it is not loud. When you are finished, you will rise refreshed and alert.

After practicing the above technique for a week, you will be ready to color and texture the ball. You can make it any color or texture you want—a silver moon or a dimpled orange, for example. But it must have a *texture* of some sort, the more complex the texture the better. Hold that image for 10 or more minutes during your 20-minute practice. Each day find a different ball-shaped object in your daily routine with texture that you can use in your visualization.

For the third week, visualize a cube. See it from all sides by very slowly rotating it from various directions and angles. Make it solid the first day and hollow or transparent the second day. The third day give it a more dimensional quality, such as dividing it into eight cubic sections with white intersecting lines. The fourth day give it 27 sections or nine faces per side. Then each succeeding day divide the cube until there are too many smaller cubes to count. But don't count any of the cubes, just see them.

By the fourth week, you will be ready to "imprint." You can skip all of the above steps. In good light, gaze (with fixed intent) unblinking at the first detailed lock illustrations in this book. (If you wear glasses, leave them on.) Start with Figure 2A or 3E. Gaze for as long as you can—at least three to five minutes—or until your eyes water and obscure your view. Then, remove your glasses, close your eyes, and gently cover them with your palms, making a slight vacuum with your eye sockets. View the negative image against your closed eyelids. Hold it for as long as you can. The following day, imprint the next detailed lock in the series. Imprint no more than one lock per day until you have viewed all 20 keyhole locks detailed in this manual. This will help to commit each lock to memory.

Should you have to pick one of these locks, occasionally close your eyes and remember the above technique. Simultaneously relax all your muscles (except your fingers, of course) and "see" the lock before your closed eyes. Having imprinted the "X-ray" illustrations of this book, you will have a clear, almost mystical view of the inner workings of the lock that you are picking. You will "see" each tumbler move into place as you pick it. Generally, the more practiced you are at visualization, the better puzzle and problem solver you will become.

ALARM SWITCH LOCKS

Because of their high-security nature, a lot of these new

locking systems are used as switch locks for various machinery and alarm circuits. Nowadays, with infrared motion detectors, perimeter switch systems, and a varying host of microprocessing and laser systems, one cannot just walk into secured premises without making a big noise. But behind all of these systems—and the kingpin to their effectiveness—is the switch lock. Each burglar alarm system has to be able to be turned on and off by the owner. This convenience has a price, though, as the switch lock can be picked like any other lock.

CARRYING LOCK PICKS

Many people have asked me about the legal right to carry lock picks on their person, and I wish that I could answer with a definitive yes or no. The problem is that each state in the union has its own laws. Some states are more rigid than others when it comes to the law, but in most states, one must be a qualified locksmith to have the right to carry picks. To have that right, one must take the state locksmith's test at the state capitol's office of licensing. But, there is more to locksmithing than just being good at picking locks.

If you are a lock distributor, law officer, or bona fide repossessor, you can try calling your county courthouse to speak with the county clerk. In some of the larger populated counties, they are better informed and are more willing to help you. After moving back to the state where he grew up, a friend of mine had to talk with one county clerk, three policemen, a police sergeant, and two locksmiths before he could get a straight answer. Hopefully you will not have to go through all that.

If you are not sure about your state, call your local locksmith right off the bat and ask him what it takes to legally carry your picks. You don't have to give him your name, just ask the innocent question. Tell him that you are interested in locksmithing and need to know the laws regarding carrying. Most will be happy to give you information on what you have to do to protect yourself should you be picked up by the local authorities under suspicion of burglary, or during a routine traffic stop.

By the way, it is your constitutional right to be served a search warrant before any cop can riffle through your wallet or personal belongings. But while the Fourth Amendment is supposed to protect us from search unless officers have "reasonable suspicion," that interpretation is broad—which is why there is a judicial system to sort the details out. So to avoid all that hassle, you are better off going through the hoops that your state requires.

IF ALL ELSE FAILS, PERFORM EXPLORATORY SURGERY

Another important point that should be made here is that not all locks of the same species are keyed alike. You may have success picking your practice lock, but the one out in the field may give you a conniption fit. In any case, you have a better chance of opening the one out there if you know the workings of the one in your shop.

If the lock sitting on your bench is not covered in this book, I suggest that you use your cut-off wheel and give it a good old-fashioned autopsy. Sometimes that's the best way to find out how the system works. I suggest that you carefully cut it length-wise above and below the cylinder for best viewing. Be careful not to dissect your finger or hand in the process—you already know how they work. Most locks though, come right apart with either a rear nut, a side-mounted set screw or a roll pin that can be punched out with the proper-sized pin punch.

There is nothing like a good challenge to keep the senses and one's lock-picking skills fresh and alive. That is another reason why I hope you will enjoy reading and using this book. But before we can learn how to pick these new high-security locks, we will need some shiny, brand spanking new tools—which just so happen to be covered in the first chapter of this book.

1.   *Pick Guns*, John Minnery, Paladin Press.
2.   The pin tumbler lock originated in ancient Egypt around 4.5 thousand years ago and was made of wood. The modern brass pin tumbler lock started its extensive use around the turn of the last century.
3.   See example in *Secrets of Lock Picking*, p. 36, Paladin Press.
4.   These pin types will be discussed in Chapter 2.

1

Tools of the Trade

A large percentage of the tools that we are about to discuss have been covered in my previous two lock-picking books,[1] and over the years they have served me well. Some of these tools have had to be slightly modified here and there, so it is important that we review them now as they will be needed to open some of the high-security locks we will be covering.

But some of these locks will require new tools—most of which I have designed as I needed them. These tools can be easily made from readily available materials. In the same way, you should also explore different and better tools to open these locks, as many household items can be employed. But first, let's dispel some myths about what is considered the best lock-picking tool around.

PICK GUNS

Many readers write me asking about pick guns. I have used a few pick guns, and some work better than others. But overall, they have three inherent problems: they may require an AC power source or batteries, they are too big and bulky to carry on your person, and in just seconds they can add decades of wear to the springs, pins, or wafers of a lock.

The principle on which they work is an age-old trick in the locksmith trade of opening cylinder locks by "rapping." It is done by applying light tension-wrench pressure on the cylinder while smacking the shell with a soft-faced hammer or on the workbench. This causes an inertial force upon the lower pins to drive the upper pins high into their spring-loaded cavities. This impact allows the pins to clear the cylinder/shell shear line and the cylinder turns, unlocking the lock. This technique will not work on a door-mounted pin tumbler lock, so it was reasoned that by impacting the individual pins (or wafers) the same effect would occur.

This inspired the invention of the pick gun, which was patented by Eli Epstein in 1922 (Patent #1,403,753), but the original concept had been around for some time.[2] Since then, the pick gun has evolved from a simple spring-loaded impact tool to an electromechanical vibrator. Then came a system that uses a rotary hammer driven by a small electric motor. The latest device uses a rotary cam mechanism, also driven by a small electric motor. Though some modern manufacturers claim that their pick guns are "electronic," there actually are no electronic components in them; they are simply electric pick guns. It *is* possible to build an electronic-type pick gun by using a transistor flip-flop oscillator, driving an SCR[3] circuit to drive an electromechanical vibrator, but why go to all that trouble and expense when an electric motor or electromagnetic coil will do the same job?

In any case, the pick gun's shaft impacts the pins with enough force to cause the lock to rub shavings from the pins, making it easier to pick by hand afterwards, hence decreasing the security of the cylinder and causing key-jamming problems later on. You can tell if a pick gun was used on your lock by all the brass-filing dust in and around the keyway. You might just as well drill the cylinder with slightly more effort because it is going to need to be replaced soon anyway. Most responsible locksmiths will not use a pick gun for that reason alone unless it is an emergency, in which case the lock should be replaced.

Another disadvantage to pick guns is that they seldom work on pin tumbler locks that are mounted upside down. Since about 40 percent of these locks are mounted upside down in America and nearly 80 percent are mounted this way overseas, a pick gun becomes that much more inconvenient to have around. (Locks mounted upside-down wear out faster because tiny brass filings and dirt can fall down past the driver pins and into the springs, causing tumblers to gum up. This is a common cause of lock-outs and broken-off keys as the bottom pins fall down past shear line. Water vapor can also condense and drip down into the springs causing lock freeze-up in cold weather.)

Pick guns can be made from modified electric jigsaws, electric scissors, and even personal vibrators. ("Ah hum . . . excuse me, I do say my good man, what are you doing there, givin' the lock a jolly good time?") However, for more specific information about pick guns I recommend *Pick Guns* by John Minnery. It is very informative and interesting reading. He also invented, and includes with illustrations, an effective line of pick guns made from wire coat hangers.

So in conclusion on this subject, a pick gun of any sort (as of present-day technology) will not work on the newer high-security tumbler locks that are in extensive use

Figure 1A. The overrated pick gun will not work on high security locks. Courtesy of ESP Lock Products, LLC.

today. Only the original key or a highly skilled human hand can open them.

LOCK PICKS—THE ULTIMATE FINGER TOOLS

HPC in Chicago sells hardened steel picks stamped from stock at a pretty reasonable price. You can get them from Clark Security Products (Visit their Web site at <www.clark-security.com/sitemap.asp> for locations across the country.) Clark also carries pick guns. Please do not call them unless you are a bonded locksmith or with a law enforcement agency, as they will not send lock picks to just anybody. Some inquiries are also investigated, as I have discovered. Another good source is the ESP Lock Products Company. Write them at 375 Harvard Street, Leominster, MA 01453 for a free catalog. They make good quality picks as stamped-out ones go. They also will verify whether or not you are a bonded locksmith or cop before responding.

You can also get picks on the Internet: Try <www.lockpicks.com>. But you get what you pay for—stamped-out picks tend to break often, as they cannot be tempered like stainless steel. Also, they rust when carried on your person (from the natural moisture of the body) making a nasty reddish-brown stain in your wallet, pocket, or on the skin. So good

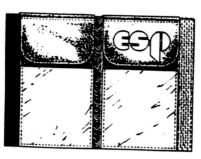

Figure 1B. Conventional lock pick sets are not adequate to handle the new high-security locking systems. Courtesy of ESP Lock Products, LLC.

lock-pick tools are hard to find and wear out rapidly, break, rust, or are just not shaped for the newer high-security locks.

Personally, I prefer hand-ground, stainless-steel picks because though they may bend, they will not break under normal use and can be bent back into shape. Also, with this tapered shaft design, the likelihood of one bending is remote (lock picks are finger tools that require delicate manipulation for proper use and should never be used with excessive force). For comfort, I put cushioned, color-coded vinyl caps over the handle ends of picks when working with high-security locks, as these locks usually take time to pick open.

All the tools that I use here can be made at home and some are covered in my first two books. It is best that you make your own. If you have stainless-steel steak knives (flat, stainless butter knives will also work) and an inexpensive grinder with cut-off wheel, you can copy off the patterns. Cut them out (inside of the line) and lightly glue the patterns on the thoroughly cleaned knives, then spray paint two to three light coats (two minutes drying time between coats) with a high-temperature paint such as black woodstove paint. Let dry 20 minutes, then carefully peel off the paper patterns with a needle and bake the knives for one hour in a 275-degree oven. When cooled, you'll have a hard, durable pattern from which to cut and grind your own professional, lifetime picks. Follow the instructions in these books and remember to cut your patterns right on the inside of the line.

THE LATEST LOCK PICKS

I have had a chance to extensively test the tools that I showed you how to make in my previous books. I have made modifications on some and invented new ones for today's locks. (Also, all picks in the illustrations of this book are shown unburnished for detail. You *must* burnish your picks before using them or they will file shavings off the tumblers and keyway and hinder picking and the lock's performance.) But let's review some of the old reliable standards as well: If

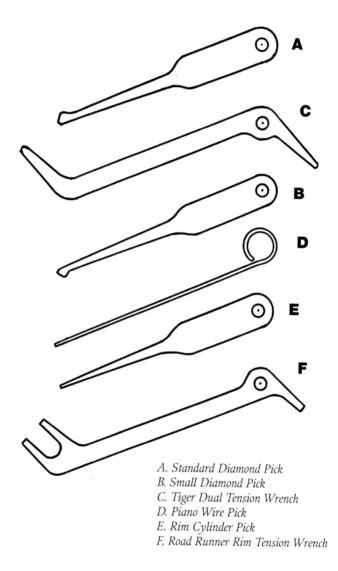

A. Standard Diamond Pick
B. Small Diamond Pick
C. Tiger Dual Tension Wrench
D. Piano Wire Pick
E. Rim Cylinder Pick
F. Road Runner Rim Tension Wrench

Figure 1C. On the next three pages are some state-of-the-art lock picks. Carefully note the inside lines as exact dimensions. We will refer back to these illustrations often.

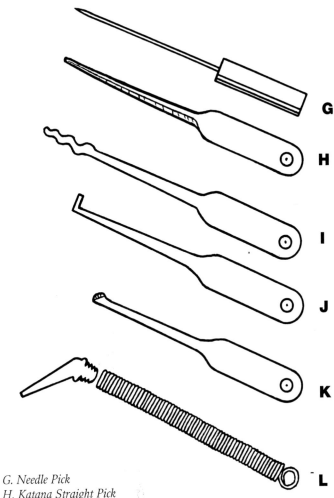

G. *Needle Pick*
H. *Katana Straight Pick*
I. *Snake Rake Pick*
J. *Scorpion Hook Pick*
K. *Monkey Twisted-Wedge Diamond Pick*
L. *White Crane Feather Touch Tension Wrench*

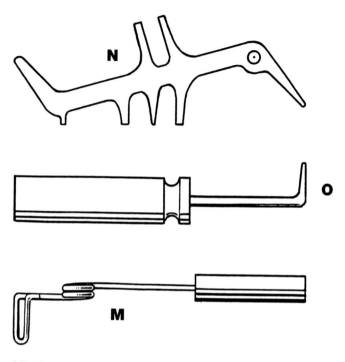

M. *Looped Feather Touch Tension Wrench*
N. *Dragon Tension Wrench*
O. *TuBar Tension Wrench*

you must carry lock picks, for practical reasons I recommend the CIA Special: the standard diamond pick ("A") and the Tiger dual tension wrench ("C"). These two tools are all I ever carry: They will get you into 70 percent of the keyhole locks used today. The standard diamond pick ("A") will work on virtually any pin or wafer tumbler lock. I have even used it to open a suitcase lever lock. In addition, the small diamond pick ("B") is used for small pin tumbler padlocks and some tight keyways—but should never be used on standard pin tumbler locks with stiff cylinders.

The Tiger dual tension wrench ("C") features a narrow tongue for all pin tumbler house and padlocks. It can center-fix on double wafer lock cylinders giving it a greater range of use. Because of its width, it can also wedge into the groove of most rim cylinder locks. The wide tongue is used for automotive and large tumbler locks. If you are a locksmith, you will appreciate the value and convenience of this set. Remember, all tools are shown exact size inside of the lines. Always wear safety glasses when making tools!

CIA SPECIAL

A. **Standard Diamond Pick:** This tool has been around for almost a century and is used on the popular pin tumbler lock to gently pry up the pins to their breaking point so that the cylinder may turn. Our modern version is simple; the unique design lends to easy movement within the lock while sporting a small, raised, flat surface to contact the individual pins. This tool is the primary pick for nearly all standard pin tumbler house locks. It can also be used on double wafer tumbler locks, but the pick must be withdrawn and reversed to work both sets of tumblers (see *Secrets of Lock Picking*). It is a direct pattern of the one that I carried and used for 17 years, which doesn't show a bit of wear and is as straight as the day I ground it (.030″ stock).

B. **Small Diamond Pick:** A scaled-down version of the above for small pin tumbler locks such as padlocks (Master); file cabinets (Chicago, Curtis); gaming machines (Fort, Hudson); discus mushroom pin tumbler padlocks (Abus); and even wafer desk drawer locks (Eagle, Welch); and various other applications where good security is required within a small space. Use .030″ stock.

C. **Tiger Dual Tension Wrench:** A good all-around wrench (American, all automotive, Chicago, Corbin, Illinois, Master, Quikset, Russwin, Schlage, Weiser, Yale, etc.— some high-security locks as well). This tool is also patterned from the one I carried for 17 years. But before I could copy it, I had to straighten the wide blade. I was amazed by how readily it straightened. It took some careful force in a small vise, but it came out strong and flat;

this stuff is tough. See above for earlier comments on this tool. Use .040" thick stock.

SERVICEMAN'S TOOL BOX

D. **Piano Wire Pick:** .030" to .035" diameter stainless steel wire (see conversion chart at end of chapter) with flat, very lightly burnished end for picking radial pin (rim cylinder) locks.

E. **Rim Cylinder Pick:** Used to depress the pins on radial pin tumbler locks (Ace, Gem, etc.) such as on vending and arcade machines. Its square-faced tip seats firmly on the surface of older pins. Even at an angle, however, this tends to leave scratch marks on the pins, so use this tool as squarely as possible. Use .030" thick stock.

F. **Road Runner Rim Tension Wrench** (with Double Wafer Wrench on the other end): The single prong is cut to fit nicely into most rim cylinder locks (Ace, Gem). The double end is used to get a grip on double wafer tumbler locks (Schlage, Chicago). This tool should be .043" to .045" thick. Burnish the prongs only slightly so that they grip the cylinder better.

G. **Needle Pick:** Detailed in Chapter 4.

H. **Katana Straight Pick:** This pick is used on multiple-row pin tumbler locks and made so that one-half of the tool is patterned on a steak-knife blade with the knife's edge running along the bottom edge of the pick. Or, you can lay it out and make the tool on flat stock of .030" to .035" thick stainless and grind an edge along its length. Note the slight upward curve of the blade. Be sure to burnish off any and all sharp edges on the tool and round off the tip. It should slip smoothly and comfortably through your fingers when you are finished making it. The tool must be able to slip in and out of a cylinder without snagging and with little effort.

I. **Snake Rake Pick:** Our special design was inspired by the dampened sine-wave form of matter-in-motion and glides across pin tumblers, causing them to virtually oscillate into position with the right tension wrench pressure. For medium security house locks (Ilco, Quikset) and cylinders with larger keyways. Also used for the ultra-high security ASSA Desmo lock. Use .035" or less stock.

J. **Scorpion Hook Pick:** For probing larger pin tumbler locks used in old United States jails and prisons. Also, lever and warded locks. Here used as a tension wrench for the high security radial pin Van lock. Use .035" stock.

SPECIALTY PICKS

K. **Monkey Twisted-Wedge Diamond Pick:** A standard .030" diamond pick with a new twist—the tip, that is. Its angle of approach is precision ground to cause pins to rotate. For high-security locks (such as those from Medeco) whose chiseled-tipped pins not only have to rise to break with the cylinder, but have to turn as well. It has been improved by grinding the leading edge of the tool at a 30-degree angle, then burnished to prevent pin scraping, facilitating a smoother rotating action on the pins as they are picked. (So-named because monkeys are the only animals that can manipulate objects within a tight, confined opening.)

L. **White Crane Feather Touch Tension Wrench:** "The yielding hand often opens the way." We find this to be true. Some cylinders (American, Corbin, Russwin, Sargent, and Yale) sport mushroom or spool-shaped pins that "break" too soon when being picked. This wrench allows you to apply only a light, constant pressure upon the cylinder so that these pins can be jostled into place to open the lock. You can pop spool and mushroom pin tumbler locks with ease using this tool as it drives the cylinder without jamming the pins while picking. Our design is made with a stainless steel point, anchored into a special stainless steel spring with the perfect force-to-distance tension ratio required to pop high-security locks made by Medeco and ASSA.

Cut insert (tip) from .035" stainless steel stock leaving

threads for last. Mount tip securely in vise and carefully file the threads with a small triangular V-notching file. Leave extra material on the threads as each spring is a slightly different size. You should custom-fit this piece to the spring you will be using. Note that threads are staggered between each side. (Do not de-burr threads.) Then screw the special spring onto the insert up to the stop collar. Once on, the spring cannot be removed unless you cut it, so be sure that the end of the spring is burnished and de-burred first to prevent snagging on clothing and self.

You can order your stainless steel spring(s) from Century Spring Corporation, P.O. Box 15287, Los Angeles, CA 90017, <www.centuryspring.com> for $6.00 each. There is a $30 minimum order, so order five different springs for a variety of tensions to work the varioius locks detailed in this book:

Lock	Spring Rate	Wire Diameter	Part #
KABA	.71	.022"	80171S
Medeco	1.1	.024"	80183S
Corbin, Russwin, Yale	1.7	.026"	80196S
Ruko	1.7	"	"
ASSA Twin 6000	1.7	"	"
ASSA X-10	3.2	.029"	80208S
ASSA Desmo	4.5	.031"	80221S

Use an *extension*-type spring with a free-length of 2.5 inches. You may experiment with different rates for each lock. The spring rate that works best for me might not be right for you. I have large hands, so I tend to use too much pressure on the wrench. If you have smaller hands, try a higher spring rate (stiffer wrench). If I had to choose which White Crane tension wrench to carry, it would be the 1.7 and 1.1 in that order.

M. Looped Feather Touch Tension Wrench: This has been a standard high-security tool in the industry since the

1950s. Even today I find this tool very effective, though a little too difficult to carry on person as it is a three-dimensional device. The Crane is also three-dimensional, but in a comfortable, round sort of way; it is easy to carry close to the person. The looped wrench must not be crushed or otherwise bent by accident, as that would render it quite ineffective. Still, to this day, this tool is in my arsenal of high-security lock picks. It has proven itself time and again.

Mine is made of stainless steel piano wire with a diameter of .031" and bent tightly into two full loops around a .250" diameter steel rod held in a vise. The end loop that goes into the keyway is .500" long with a .125"-wide tongue. You may wrap the end of the tongue wire back around the shaft and clip it off short. Burnish this end until there's no threat of snagging on fingers or clothing. My original looped Feather Touch was carefully brazed between the loop and shaft as is illustrated. However, since brazing can detemper stainless (and most other metals), it is best to wrap the end of the wire around the shaft. The handle end, you may finish as you wish. I flattened that end with hammer and anvil to keep it from spinning within its handle, then heated that end with a cigarette lighter and forced it into a round plastic rod about .250" in diameter as a handle. Center-mark the plastic rod for a guide to wire placement. This will give you a well-centered handle for this tool. Remember to wear safety glasses when making this or any other tool.

N. Dragon Tension Wrench: I mention this tool again because it is so versatile. This design is improved with a Van Lock tension wrench tab for the Dragon's very hind leg. This tool though, will work on virtually any cylinder lock: The Dragon's "head" and "tail" are basically the Tiger dual tension wrench ("C") shown on p. 18. But this tool also has three built-in spanner wrenches that grip the cylinders of the three major radial pin lock types: Ace, Gem, Chicago, and all other large radial pin locks used on the older vending machines. The Dragon's snout can also hold other rim cylinders. Use .035" stock. The "wings" are a fourth spanner set used to turn double wafer cylinders.

O. TuBar Tension Wrench: Detailed in Chapter 3.

AUXILIARY EQUIPMENT

Magnifier: When making tools (or inspecting locks) I use a headband Opti-Visor (Model DA-3 or newer), an Optical Glass Binocular Magnifier so as to see the lines very clearly. It makes a world of difference when doing precise work. They fit comfortably over glasses, too. I find the best lens for me is the #3, as the focal length comes out to 14 inches. I often wear them when picking a new and difficult lock. Don't wear them while cutting a tool though, as one needs wider depth perception to work safely with power tools. Contact Donegan Optical Company by mail at P.O. Box 14308, Lenexa, KS 66285-4308 or visit their Web site at <www.doneganoptical.com> for pricing or free catalog.

Penlight: A good penlight is also very important. For just a few dollars, Radio Shack sells a very convenient penlight that uses a fiber-optic rod for looking into tight places.

The best affordable penlight system for looking into keyholes is the Nite Ize fiber-optic adapter. It fits over the end of the 7" and 20" (AA size) Mini-Maglite. A smaller version is available for the 4.5" and 20" (AAA size) Mini-Maglites. Each unit is less than $6 and available at your local Wal-Mart. Or, you may visit their Web site at <www.niteize.com> for a catalog.

Figure 1D. The Opti-Visor helps the locksmith work with fine parts and to make specialized lock picks.

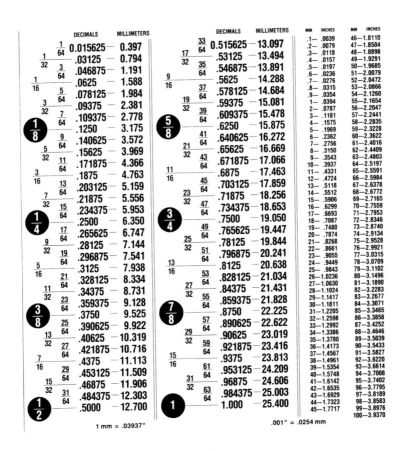

Figure 1E. Fraction to decimal conversion chart.

1. *Secrets of Lock Picking* and *Advanced Lock Picking Secrets*, both published by Paladin Press.
2. *Pick Guns*, John Minnery, Paladin Press.
3. Invented in 1957 at General Electric to control 30+ amperes of current, an SCR is a "silicon controlled rectifier" or, simply put, a solid-state (having no moving parts) power switch where a small electrical current can control a much larger current in either an "on" or "off" mode for inductive loads such as motors and relays. Some SCRs are brutes and can switch thousands of amps. (By comparison, a 100-watt light bulb draws just under 1 amp.) But for here, much smaller versions of this device are available.

Spooled/Mushroom Pin Tumbler Locks

This chapter is a short review of the pin tumbler lock. The "high security" aspect of this chapter involves the pins that can make this lock a formidable challenge to even the most experienced lock picker.

Spool and mushroom driver pin tumblers have been around for a long time and have proven to be the best security features that a pin tumbler lock can possess. Invented by the Yale Lock Company, these pins can make picking pin tumbler locks a tiresome experience.

SPOOL PINS

Spool pins were the first to be utilized in pin tumbler cylinders and they are simple in design. When a pin is being picked (or raised by an improper key), the cylinder is forced by the tension wrench to align in the gap of the spool with the leading inner edge of the lock's shell, jamming any further attempts to turn the cylinder. Corbin and Russwin relied heavily on these pins for their security from the 1930s

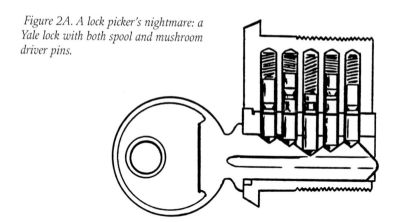

Figure 2A. A lock picker's nightmare: a Yale lock with both spool and mushroom driver pins.

through '60s. These locks were used extensively on bank doors and other high-risk areas where sums of money or valuables were at stake. With the invention of the Feather Touch tension wrench in the 1940s, which required more skill to use, the mighty spool pin was brought down to being only a minor nuisance to the professional lock picker.

MUSHROOM PINS

These pins were designed and employed to foil pick gun attacks and manual picking in particular. Because of their

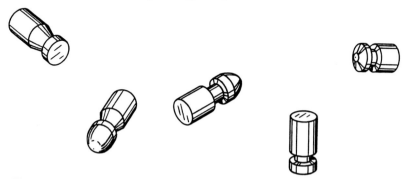

Figure 2B. High security top driver pins through the years (from left to right): The ever popular Yale mushroom pin; an early Sargent mushroom pin; an early Russwin mushroom pin; a modern, single-grooved spool pin; and the latest—an ASSA V-10 mushroom pin.

shape, mushroom pins are a devious ploy against the determined thief. This is why: As the bottom pins are raised, the force from the tension wrench causes the cylinder to turn at the first sign of relief against the raised, mushroom pin. There is no clear-cut distinction of a breaking point, as with spool pins. Rather, when the cylinder starts to give way to the wrench, one feels that he has actually picked the lock—until the cylinder stops dead about 15 to 20 degrees later. To the inexperienced lock picker this can be a very frustrating experience. But in fact, these pins cannot be picked one at a time as with a standard pin tumbler lock. In most cases, the sloppier the picking process (with a light, steady wrench torque), the better chance one has of popping a mushroom-pin lock.

Pick guns seldom work with mushroom driver pins as these pins must be free to rise under the gun's vibratory forces—which cannot happen even with the slightest of tension wrench torque.

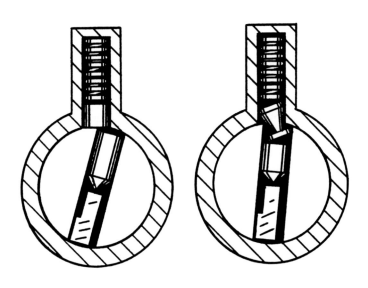

Figure 2C. Standard pin tumbler cylinder (left) and mushroom pin tumbler cylinder.

THE ABUS DISKUS PADLOCK

Because of its small keyway and tough nature, the ABUS Diskus padlock is generally considered a high-security lock. American-made Yale mushroom pins are the highlight of this German-made marvel, which has been distributed worldwide for more than 40 years and in the United States for at least 25 years.[1] I mentioned this lock briefly in *Advanced Lock Picking Secrets*, however, this German bomb has since evolved into one of the most pick-resistant padlocks on the market. (I must have pissed them off.)

Figure 2D. The ABUS Diskus Padlock shown closed and open.

This "Urban Tough" breed of lock has a stainless steel body and shackle. Note the upside-down keyway. Most European pin tumbler locks have their cylinders mounted upside down—I am not sure why (other than to foil pick-gun attacks). But this seems to me that it would cause more problems than not. However, with the ABUS padlock, this works to its advantage. Because of its enclosed shackle, you can't swing the lock around to pick it properly like most other padlocks. So you are forced to pick it upside down. The enclosed shackle rotates within the Diskus body when the lock is unlocked, so there is no shackle spring. This, however, is to the lock picker's advantage; less force is needed to pop the cylinder once you do get the mushroom pins in proper place.

But that is a minor advantage. The tight, corrugated keyway alone totally eliminates attacks by pick guns and all but the thinnest of diamond picks. A thin, small diamond pick is the only hope one has of opening the lock.

This lock now carries five pins (all mushroom-top pins) and a tighter keyway than 20 years ago. My standard diamond pick ("A") was too large to get into the tight keyway so I had to go to the smaller diamond pick ("B"). The Tiger wrench ("C") must mount further out on its narrow point to grip the cylinder. This told me right away that I was in trouble. I finally went to the White Crane Feather Touch wrench and settled down for a long haul. After 25 minutes of fiddling around, I managed to get my sample lock open. Most of my time was spent trying to get into a comfortable position to pick it.

ABUS makes a variety of other pin tumbler padlocks. The steel laminated 41 and 45 Series uses four mushroom pins; the brass 55 and 55M Series uses four standard pins; the brass 65 Series uses five mushroom pins; the 36 and 37 Series "Granit" uses "pick-proof" seven-disc tumblers. The 88 Series ABUS also use seven-disc tumblers using the same spacing as the Abloy disc tumbler lock. It is very similar to the Abloy in many other ways as well. We will discuss keyed disc tumbler locks in Chapter 9.

The ABUS "Convertible" 83/45 Z-bar (a retaining piece at the rear of the cylinder) will hold an IC (interchangeable core) that can be keyed to your house, so don't be surprised if you encounter an Arrow, Corbin, Kwikset, Russwin, Sargent, Schlage, Weiser-Falcon, or Yale keyway and pins inside this brass padlock.

Pick resistance: The ABUS Diskus padlock is the only lock we are concerned with here. For the money, it is one of the best padlocks on the market and I rate this pain-in-the-wazoo a **7.5.**

---

1. An American version of this lock is made by Federal Lock.

3

Radial Pin Tumbler Locks

The radial pin tumbler lock was covered in my first two books, previously referred to by the more common name of "tubular rim cylinder" or "tube-rim" locks. However, with further experience on my part and new advances in this style of lock, I thought this would be a good opportunity to expand on these high-security locks. Let's review this venerable modified pin tumbler mechanism.

INTERNAL PLUG

The standard of the vending-machine era for the last 30+ years, these familiar seven-pin tube-key locks have been subject to assault from drills, hole saws, hammers, punches, and even sophisticated picking techniques.[1] However, it is still one of the best security devices available for its price.

THE GEMATIC RADIAL PIN TUMBLER

One of the latest versions of radial pin tumbler locks uses master keyed pin tumblers. This allows the person with the master control key to exclude a particular key (for example, to guard against the use of a key that's been lost or stolen). Fort Lock's Gematic has eight pins, but one master control key can set the cylinder so that it will only accept one out of eight different keys. This allows a supervisor to set up the lock so that one select employee can open it (boggles the brain). The customer can also change the key code up to eight times. Since there are extra dividing cuts on the pins, it makes picking these locks easier than the standard radial pin tumbler. Priced at around $13 each and $2 per key, this lock is rated at **7.0.**

Though radial pin tumbler locks can be picked with skill and patience—qualities most burglars lack—they still require too much time, as every 45-degree turn of the cylinder means that the lock must be picked again. Some of the older vending machines use a T-handle, which takes several 360-degree turns to unscrew and release the vending machine's door. That's about 42 pickings of a seven-pin tumbler lock—with a spanner tension wrench that

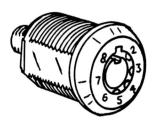

Figure 3A. Fort Lock's Gematic has up to eight key-code changes. Master keying the radial pin tumbler means more cuts in the pins, which increases the chances of picking the lock open.

tends to fly off the plug (cylinder). We're talking major stress here. The new T-handles pop out once the lock is unlocked, and turn right just 180 degrees. But the locks tend to have higher security cylinders such as KABA, Medecos, or Abloy. We'll discuss these locks later in the book.

Again, as explained in my previous work, a tension wrench must be affixed to the cylinder plug (the most difficult task in picking this lock, aside from the time involved) and secured so as to affect a slight torque upon it. Then, each pin must be

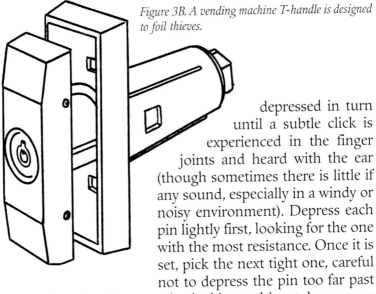

Figure 3B. A vending machine T-handle is designed to foil thieves.

depressed in turn until a subtle click is experienced in the finger joints and heard with the ear (though sometimes there is little if any sound, especially in a windy or noisy environment). Depress each pin lightly first, looking for the one with the most resistance. Once it is set, pick the next tight one, careful not to depress the pin too far past its shear line. In this way, the lock's machine tolerance, or "slop," can be taken advantage of.

In the newer T-handles, these cylinders need only to turn 90 to 120 degrees, which means that you must still pick them at least two or three times. This problem can be overcome with various locksmiths' rim cylinder pick tools (one of which I designed myself). But I cannot discuss these here as little skill is involved and such tools in the hands of an unscrupulous few would create much grief and condemn the radial pin tumbler lock into extinction.

The tension wrench direction depends on the set-up. There is a slot between the plug and shell that allows the key to be inserted into the lock. (See switch lock configuration chart on p. 38.)

Now, 90 to 120 degrees (usually to the right) there is another slot, but it is only in the outer shell. This is where the key is removed from the lock once it is turned to the unlocked position. Generally, if an exit slot is to the right, pick right. If left, go left. Typically, all Chicago Lock Company's Ace, Ace 2, and Ace Change-Matics radial pin tumbler locks

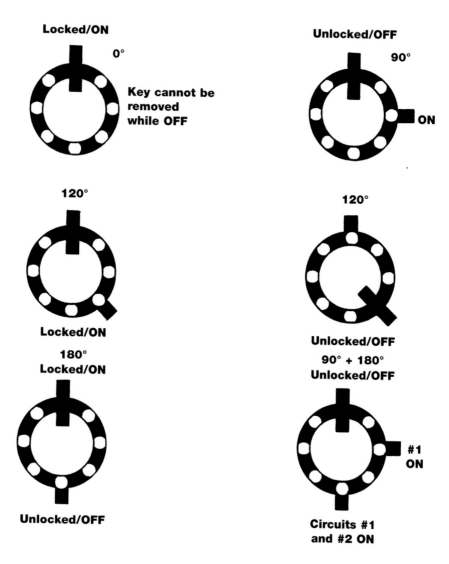

Figure 3C. The most common configurations of radial pin tumbler switch-locks.

unlock to the right, or clockwise. The Fort Lock Company's Gem, Gematic, and Apex also follow this rule. Some cheap foreign locks may not, but in every other way, those locks pick the same.

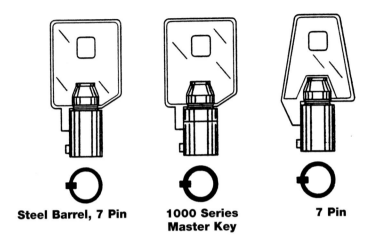

Steel Barrel, 7 Pin   **1000 Series**   **7 Pin**
                              Master Key

Figure 3D. Barrel or "tube" key blanks: Despite efforts to secure the keyway, they all have the same O.D. (outer diameter) plug dimension, making a standard tension wrench possible.

Pick resistance: Even though each pin is exposed to the lock picker and the cylinder is relatively easy to grab hold of, because of the time involved I rate these types of radial pin tumbler locks at **7.5**. These locks typically run around $9.

But, if that's not enough, other companies have developed a higher degree of quality with lower machine tolerances—tighter locks—and so a different approach to the same principle.

INTERNAL PLUG—TUBE PIN

All radial pin tumbler locks can be used for alarm switches. But this next lock—the radial tube pin tumbler—brought lock picking to a higher level of tedium and is often used to thwart the turning off of burglar alarm systems by the intruder.

The first time I encountered this piece of work made by the Chicago Lock Co., I was very impressed—I still am. However, since there is more stuff in there, there's a little more room to get a pick onto both the seven pins and the four individual tubes. With 11 total pins, that's a whole lot of

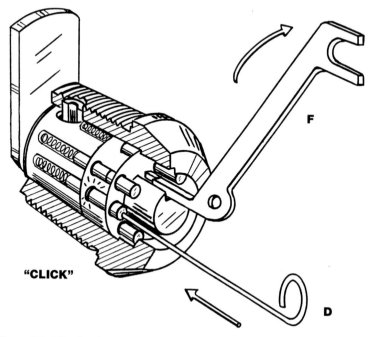

"CLICK"

Figure 3E. The Roadrunner ("F") and the piano wire pick are shown opening a radial pin tumbler lock. First pick the pin that binds the most, then pick subsequent pins.

picking. Still, you have to pick the lock three or four times to shut off the switch at the back of the lock.

I must make a correction here: on page 15 of *Advanced Lock Picking Secrets* I stated that all the round (solid) pins had to be picked first. Somehow I got that backwards while writing it. The tube pins must be picked first, before any round pins can be set to their shear line as they are, obviously, the first pins to encounter the shear line between the cylinder and shell.

Pick resistance: These cylinders are just a little more hassle to open so I rated them, in general, at **8**. This lock is no longer in production and has been replaced by the Chicago TuBar mentioned at the end of this chapter.

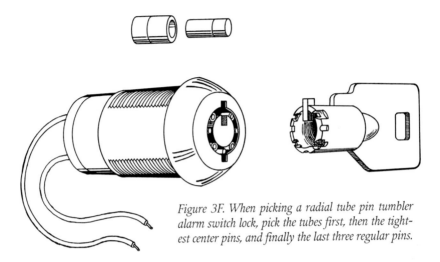

Figure 3F. When picking a radial tube pin tumbler alarm switch lock, pick the tubes first, then the tightest center pins, and finally the last three regular pins.

EXTERNAL PLUG

The Van Lock Company has a unique approach to modern security with its custom, handmade radial pin tumbler locks. They have stainless steel pins in flush-mounted faces designed to resist pipe wrenching, punching, and pulling from unguarded vending machines. These radial locks have their cylinder (plug) on the outside rim of the lock, as opposed to the inside like the older Gem, Ace, and other styles shown above. The manufacturer claims that they cannot be picked because ". . . pick tools cannot get to the pins." I find these locks are still vulnerable to the pick, maybe even more so than the standard radial pin lock. Let's see why:

First off, I call this an external plug radial pin tumbler not because the plug is exposed to the outside rim of the lock, but because the pins are inside the plug. The brass cylinder face rotates with the flush stainless steel pins. The plug itself is enclosed around its circumference by the edge of the shell. This edge is also machined to accept the key rim as if it were the single thread of a fruit jar. Once the key is engaged to the lock and turned a bit, it cannot be removed, even after unlocking the lock 120 degrees later. To do so without this

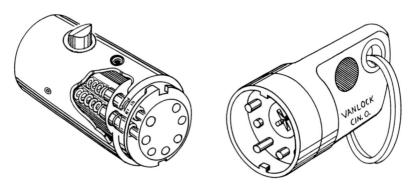

Figure 3G. The punch, pull, and drill resistant Van lock with its key: surrounding the pins with the plug. Special tools ("E" and "J") are needed to pick this high-security lock.

engagement would set the surface pins to the wrong back pins, meaning that the key would have to be re-engaged at that very position to continue to unlock the lock. (In fact, this principle is exploited by Fort Lock's Gematic re-keyable rim cylinder lock mentioned at the beginning of this chapter.)

The 120 degrees, by the way, means that the surface pins must cross the spring-loaded drivers beneath them three times, which means the lock would have to be picked three times to bring down the spring-loaded catch (called the "locking dog") sticking up at the back of the cylinder. This cylinder is interchangeable and fits within the T-handle. The T-handle could then be turned to open the door of the vending machine.

Though machined to very tight tolerances, these locks work under the same principle as all other tube key locks: five to nine (seven in this case) pins must be individually depressed until a click is heard and/or felt before the cylinder can be turned to unlock the lock. But in this case, the spanner tension wrench can go on the outside of the lock face instead of the inside. This brings the pins right out front making them easier to get to. In a way, the Van lock is almost easier to pick because of that feature alone. And because the wrench is not on the inside of the cylinder restricting the motion of the pick, it's a cakewalk: there is no inside edge of

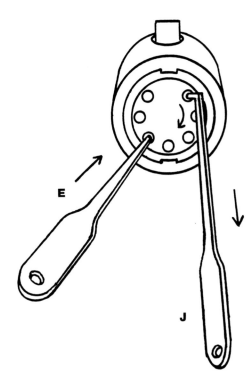

Figure 3H. Picking the Van lock: Pull or push down on the cylinder in a pinhole that breaks deep for rotary force while picking the rest of the pins.

the outer shell to scrape and drag against the wrench. It is easy to get a grip on this cylinder; apparently this was overlooked by Van. Here's how it's done: First, you cannot really use a regular tubular rim spanner wrench; it just won't work because there is not enough room between the tight plug and shell. Instead, we use an L-shaped tension wrench ("J") designed for this job. (See exact-size template.) The L-wrench is also a right-angled straight pick used to depress one of the pins, after which it remains in that pin hole to hold the plug. Find the pin that breaks deep enough so that you can also use the L-wrench to *pull* down on the plug (you may use your left hand to gently *push* the plug in a downward motion). This means that you would be better off looking for that pin in either the 1, 3, or 5 o'clock position. While gently pulling down (clockwise) with your L-wrench, depress the other pins with a standard rim pick in your left hand as if you were picking an Ace or Gem radial pin tumbler. Search for the pin with the most resistance and depress it to breaking the shear line of the plug. Find the next stiff pin and depress it, being careful not to depress any pin too low. All the while, maintain a light torque on the plug with the L-wrench.

As the cylinder begins to bind further against the pins, you may have to lighten up on the tension just a hair, but not too much. Make sure the pin you are depressing with the L-wrench is not being pushed down too deep.

Just remember, like all other radial pin tumbler locks, you will have to pick it three or more times. Also, if you do not return the plug to the locked position, the key will not operate the cylinder. This lock sells for about $15 plus $5 a key.

Pick resistance: Picking the vending-machine mounted Van lock is another story as the cylinder face is set below the surface of the T-handle, putting the tension wrench at an awkward angle. I rate this lock at a respectable **8.5**.

THE TUBAR

Recently, I had the opportunity to pick a TuBar. Invented by Robert L. Steinbach (Patent #4,446,709, 1984) for the Chicago Lock Co., this lock is used on utility cabinets, as switch locks, and on vending machines. It is advertised as ". . . the ultimate in resistance to surreptitious entry." The wording alone was enough to interest me. I just had to get this lock.

This dual side-bar eight-pin tumbler uses two rows of four pins with a side bar on each row. The pins are arranged with their ends facing the keyhole opening in two sets of four. At first glance, one would think that it is an odd version of a radial cylinder or tube rim lock, if not for the pin arrangement. It is anything but that. Though this lock is similar to a radial pin tumbler, the pins are not placed in a circular pattern. If you're a determined lock picker and know your locks, just looking down the keyhole will give rise to despair.

On the outer edge of the brass cylinder (9) (within the lock but above each row of pins) is a half-moon shaped plate (7) with a notch balancing a tapered side-bar (8) riding in a groove along the length of the cylinder. This is a double side-bar quasi-radial pin tumbler lock.

This lock sports hardened stainless steel spool pins (5).

Figure 31. Chicago Lock's TuBar is in a class of its own with eight spooled pins and two side-bars—but its pins are radially exposed. Note the hefty key to overcome the "stiffness" of the lock.

1. Steel cylinder shell
2. Anti-pick isolation plug
3. Centering pin
4. Centering pin spring
5. Spool pin tumbler
6. Tumbler spring
7. Side-bar yoke
8. Side-bar
9. Cylinder (plug)
10. Cylinder housing
11. Switch assembly

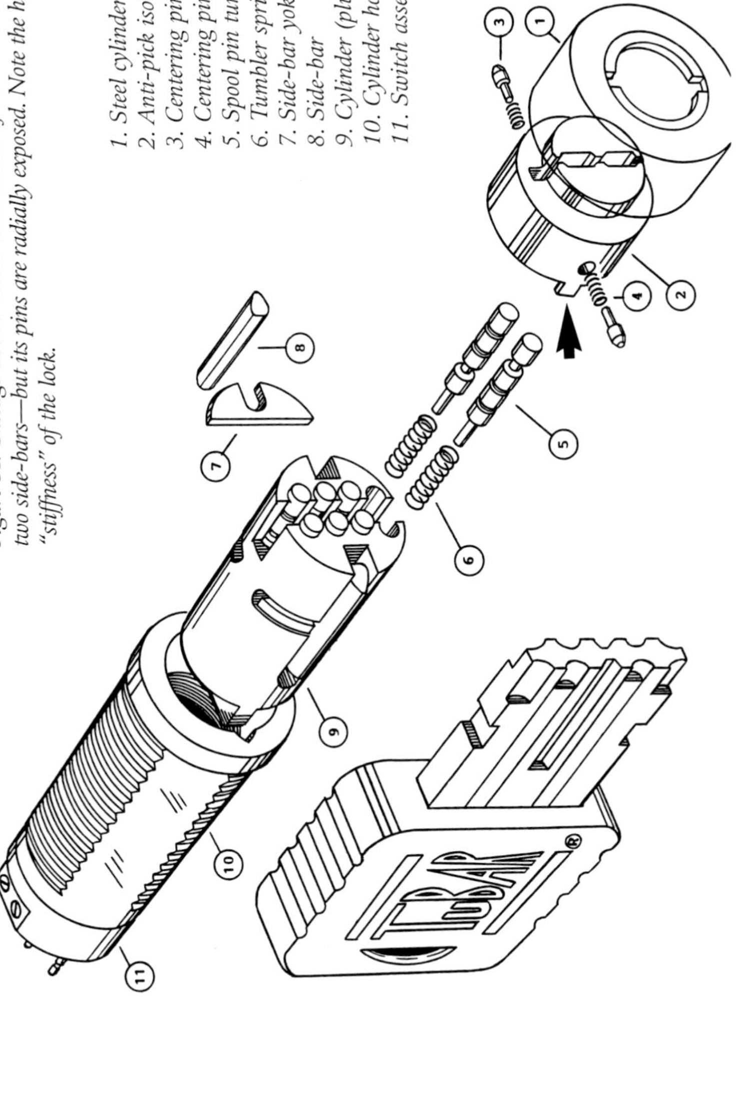

My stainless steel pick didn't even leave a mark on them, so forget about drilling out the cylinder. Also, there is a circular stainless-steel drill-proof plate (not shown) with a keyhole opening in the center. (This plate also helps to prevent drilling.) The pins are one solid piece with a heavy groove girdling the middle so that the flat side of the half-moon side-bar "yoke" can fall into it. Furthermore, each pin has two shallow fake grooves and one deep real groove, reminiscent of the old Russwin spool pin. In Figure 3I, two of the eight pins shown have the fake grooves above and below the heavy, real groove. The dissected lock that I picked has the real groove in the middle on all eight pins—but this is not the norm. My other TuBar picked with deep and shallow breaking pins. There are three different positions on each pin, and two out of three of them are "fake." The "fake" grooves seem to have a lot less relief than the real grooves, so you can use a little more force on the tension wrench than you would a standard pin tumbler lock. However, having only three different pins in an eight-pin lock limits the possible key combinations to only 6,561 (3 to the 8th power). But that doesn't matter—this lock's a bitch to pick anyway.

Unlike regular side-bar locks, this cylinder requires a stiff tension wrench. But the keyway is full of pins, so the only way to get a grip on this cylinder is in the center of the keyway. However, when the narrow tip of my Tiger dual tension wrench was placed down into the center of the keyway, it blocked the four center pins. I finally gave up picking this lock because none of the pins would stick or hold to their shear lines.

Now, you may wonder why we don't use a Feather Touch tension wrench on the little monster. The front keyhole plug (2) holds two spring-loaded pins (3), one on each side. These "centering" pins do not need to be picked—they rest in a groove on the left and right inner sides of the lock housing wall (10) and act as an added resistance to the turning of the cylinder, rendering Feather Touch tension wrenches useless.

I noticed that the steel side bars to the lock I had taken apart were beveled along their outside length. Even though

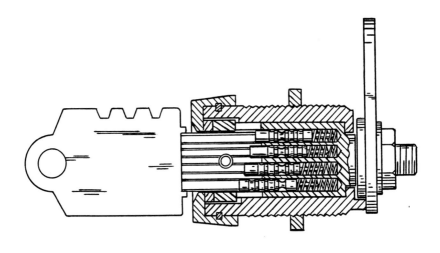

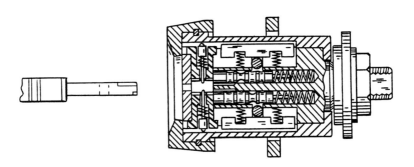

Figure 3J. Original prototype of the TuBar: Note that the side-bar springs are not necessary and roller-shaped yokes were replaced with the half-moon yokes shown in the previous illustration.

this lock is a dual side-bar, in order for the key to work properly it must compress the side bars in while turning the cylinder. So more tension wrench pressure was needed. But this also meant that you should be able to feel the tumblers as you picked them—they should stick! I realized that the problem was not enough tension wrench pressure, so I decided to design a new tension wrench. Here's how to make it:

First, take a small #1 Stanley screwdriver (Model #64-340 or the Stanley generic 2"/50mm) and grind the very tip back until it is .060" thick. Using the .032" cut-off wheel, carefully cut a slot down along the flat on both sides of the blade, being careful not to cut the slot through the blade. The tip of the screwdriver should now have an hourglass shape. The "waistline" of the hourglass should be no more than .035" thick. Next, grind down the wide sides of the blade on both shoulders until the end of the tool is .125" wide and looks like the form shown in detail in Figure 3K.

Next, put the end of the tool in a vise about 1/4 of an inch (.250") down. Tighten the vise, but not so tight as to flatten the blade. Heat with a propane torch just above the vise jaws for a minute or until it turns red and bend it to a 90-degree angle. Being careful not to burn yourself, remove it from the vise and quench in oil. Smoke will roll off the tool as it hardens itself to the new shape. You now have a TuBar hourglass tension wrench.

This hourglass tension wrench can now fit down past the front anti-Feather Touch plate and grab the cylinder. It wedges itself snugly but is just above the four center pins, allowing your straight pick to get to them. In Figure 3I, the key has a deep groove running down most of the length of the key bit. This groove allows the centering pins (3) to retract so that the anti-pick plug (2) will rotate when the proper key is inserted and turned. In the original patent illustration, redrawn for Figure 3J, this is accomplished with a hole in the side of the key. This, however, must have caused problems and the hole was replaced by the deep groove. This is the lucky break that a lockmith needs to open this lock.

The purpose for the centering pins is to prevent a rogue key from entering the lock and to discourage "center-fixing" tension wrenches.

But the centering pins cannot be so long that their ends touch in the center of the keyway or the key may not be removable—which is probably why they got rid of the key's hole. So they had to shorten the centering pins. However, the extra gap between those pins makes the lock work much better. It also allows for the use of the hourglass tension wrench. But don't get me wrong—this lock's still a bitch.

A thin (.018" to .025" thick) rim pick is used to depress each pin. I also like to use the .030" diameter piano wire picks on these locks. Either way, lightly push each pin down until you get one of them to click heavily into place. You may experience a light click just before this happens. Remember, with spool pins, light clicks don't count. You'll feel the difference once you start picking them. After getting a pin to give you a good solid click, search for another one that has lost its springiness and is ready to align. Keep your hourglass wrench firm throughout the picking process.

The cylinder turns a little bit hard, but make sure you don't push down too hard on the pins. Pick one row at a time. Find the row that the pins push down the hardest, then release the pressure on the wrench. Re-apply wrench tension and find the stiffest pin in that row and set it first. Then find the next firm pin in that row and set it. Once you have set that whole row, the following pins in the other row will set up nicely. But you must first find and set that row that causes the most relief against your tension wrench. In this way, you take advantage of the inherent tolerances (slop) in the lock. (Without some "slop," the lock would be too tight to function at all and would freeze up solid.)

Repeat this process as needed until all pins are set and then the cylinder will turn, shutting off the switch, turning the cam or dropping the dog mounted on the rear of the cylinder. You may have to play with the tension wrench a little because a pin went down too far. If you find a pin that

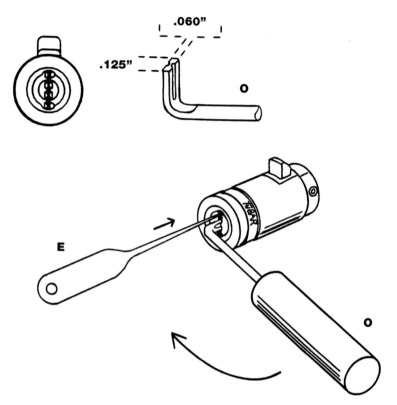

Figure 3K. Picking the TuBar lock. A firm, deep-seated tension wrench ("O") used with a light but constant turning force will set the spool pins. The wrench's special hourglass tip defeats the centering pins in TuBar's anti-pick plug.

pushes down hard, but smoothly, clear to the bottom of the cylinder, chances are it should stay up. Release tension and start again, but leave that pin alone.

Use caution when picking this lock. The anti-pick or "isolation" plug (2) has a tab (small arrow) on each side that engages the cylinder beneath. Since we are using this plug to apply rotary torque when picking this lock, do not apply too much force—just enough to bind the pins. Otherwise you will shear off those two tabs and no longer have a means to grip the cylinder behind. Only the right key will work the lock should this happen, as this plug will freely rotate once the two centering pins are overcome. This is also a telltale sign that someone has tried to pick your TuBar.

Both of my TuBar locks open to the right (clockwise). If yours do not, just remember that on any cylinder lock, if the pins will not bind or stick to the shear line you need to go the other direction with the tension wrench.

Helpful tip: In order for me to study this lock, I had to use a small, handheld Dremel tool with a cut-off wheel to bisect the rotating stainless-steel collar on the front of the lock. The collar is designed to spin so that thieves can't grab it with a pipe wrench and twist the lock out of its mounting, but once it is removed from its mounting it can be cut away by making two cuts 180 degrees apart. The isolation plug just pops out with a little prying (be careful not to lose items 3 and 4 while doing this) and the guts of the lock will spill out, exposing the toggle switch at the back of the lock. A small screwdriver may then be used to operate it.

Pick resistance: Considering the quality of machining, the steel pins with anti-pick grooves, the two side-bars, and the anti-pick plug, this is a well thought-out and very secure lock. It took me a good 40 minutes to open it after I had the right tools. I still gave it a **10.0** because of the shear audacity of the lock's damned anti-pick isolation plug. If you can't pick this lock within the first 60 minutes, or if the wrench is not fully into the keyway and slips out, the wear and stress will shear the tabs (see arrow in Figure 3I) on this plug. Then getting hold of the cylinder underneath again with any kind of tension wrench becomes quite out of the question. This is excellent security for its price—around $25 plus $5 per key.

---

1. *Advanced Lock Picking Secrets*, pp. 13-22. See the Dragon 6-'n-1 tension wrench.

Multiple Row
Pin Tumbler
Locks

Most new high-security locks use a variation of the old standard pin tumbler cylinder lock. Because it was (and still is) the most effective lock in use, the pin tumbler has evolved into a variety of complex systems, some of which may require three or more hands to pick. In some locks, one twist of the cylinder without the proper key sets off an alarm and locks down the cylinder. Nearly all of the locks discussed in this book were designed or made in Europe: Sweden, Switzerland, Denmark, Norway, or Germany. They are of high quality, which until recently made most of them too expensive or inaccessible for the average American home or business. (The large conglomerate ASSA recently bought into most of these small, innovative companies and, though it now dominates the security market, has brought the price of these high-security locks down to an affordable market price while maintaining the original company brand names. For the most part, these companies still manufacture their locks overseas.) The mechanical locks discussed in the next chapters operate with the precision of a Swiss watch.

Some of these locks are used to operate the on/off switch on burglar alarm systems and are commonly called "switch locks." It makes sense to concentrate on beefing up the pick-resistance of the alarm system rather than improving the quality of the door lock, because while a door lock can be picked, kicked in, or blown out, such treatment of the switch lock should automatically open the switch and set off the alarm, bringing the police.

THE KABA MICRO SWITCH LOCK

One such interesting switch lock is made by two Swiss companies. KABA makes the cylinder lock and EAO makes the electrical switch to fit this lock. Thus was born the KABA Micro. It is only a small, four-pin tumbler lock with a fair amount of pick time involved for its inexpensive price. The four pins are situated on the upper left side of the tight, little keyway—about .058" wide. These four pins have to be depressed to the horizontal left to release the cylinder. The switch can be wired either to turn off or on with a left turning cylinder, or a right turn.

The key is stamped stainless steel and is quite simple, being flat with no ridges milled along its working length (bit). This is a very basic dimple key with dimples for the lock's four pins on both sides so that it may enter and operate the lock right side up or upside down. For the key to be removed with the switch activated, another row of shouldered top pins lie waiting 90-degrees counterclockwise along the bottom of the keyway in Figure 4A.

I used the narrow tongue of the Tiger wrench at the bottom of the keyway, being careful not to depress the first two tumblers. I then used a thin (.018" to .022") straight rim pick to pry each pin into position with a sideways (left-to-right) motion and basically picked it like a small pin tumbler cylinder. It pops easier with a clockwise wrench turn than it does with a counterclockwise one, as the wrench tends to get in the way of the pick. Chances are, should you encounter this lock, it will open in the more difficult to pick direction.

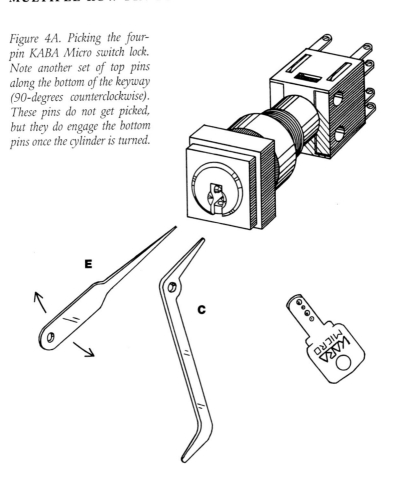

Figure 4A. Picking the four-pin KABA Micro switch lock. Note another set of top pins along the bottom of the keyway (90-degrees counterclockwise). These pins do not get picked, but they do engage the bottom pins once the cylinder is turned.

Pick resistance: This lock is actually a low-to-medium security mechanism, however, I included it here to familiarize you with the principle of right-angled pin tumbler arrays. In fact, the square housing surrounding the cylinder is plastic. But KABA makes more formidable locks, as we will soon see. This switch lock used to be employed on the old computer drives by universities and government facilities. This lock is fair security for its small size, and I rate it at **4.5**, mostly for its uniqueness.

ALPHA SLOT MACHINE LOCK

Gambling is, at best, a risky business. If you have a customer who owns a few slot machines, coin-operated bar-top video game machines, or even just a re-built, old-fashioned pinball machine, keeping the run-of-the-mill lock picker out may have been a real challenge in the past. Outside of illegal entry by strangers, sometimes employees like to dip their fingers into your pockets by using a homemade key from an impression of the key bit they made while they had access to the original key for a few moments. (The key's "bit" is the part that goes into the lock, while the "bow" is the end that attaches to the key ring.)

To make key duplication more difficult, the American company Key Devices markets their maximum security Alpha Cam or Slot Lock. Invented by Francis E. Gallagher in 1997 (patent #5,685,184), it sports 17 pin tumblers: six pins on the left side of the cylinder, six pins on top, and five pins to the right side. The maker claims over a billion possible codes. If you happen to be near a new gaming machine, chances are it has an Alpha on it. Take a gander down the keyway and you'll notice that it's full of pins. It goes a few steps further than the lock in 4A by using both sides of the key and the top edge.

The unique dimple key design allows for a small profile key to control the position of all 17 tumblers. The key is even dimpled on its uppermost edge to bring the top tumblers up to shear line. And most conveniently, the key is designed to go into and operate the lock either way. The sample key to the lock that I practiced on is covered with dimples. (It's the modern version of the old, and still used, Ford pin tumbler known as a "drunkard's key" because no matter which way you insert it into the lock, it will operate the cylinder.) It's almost hard to believe that they can get all that stuff in there, but the Alpha Slot Lock functions quite well. I am impressed with its machining and its smooth operation. However, I have noticed that some of the tumbler springs fatigue quite easily while picking this lock, allowing the pins to stick. This makes the key work rougher.

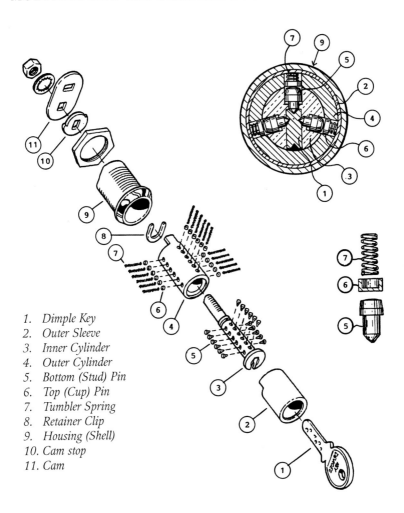

1. Dimple Key
2. Outer Sleeve
3. Inner Cylinder
4. Outer Cylinder
5. Bottom (Stud) Pin
6. Top (Cup) Pin
7. Tumbler Spring
8. Retainer Clip
9. Housing (Shell)
10. Cam stop
11. Cam

Figure 4B. The 17-pin tumbler Alpha Slot Lock. Though the tumblers travel a very short distance, there is little room for traditional lock picks in this cylinder.

To pick this lock, a thick tension wrench (like a small, bent screwdriver) or the wide end of the Tiger, must be placed at the very bottom of the keyway as if you were picking a regular wafer or small pin tumbler lock. Since the dimples in the key are shallow, be aware that the upper "cup-shaped" pins do not have far to travel to shear line. So care should be taken in the manipulation of the pick. I designed the Katana straight pick ("H") for this lock because you can gently teeter it vertically to engage the top pins, as well as rock it from side-to-side to set the left and right pins. Remember that there is very little space for driver pins and springs, so the pins do not have to be depressed very far. In fact, this is also part of its security. Not only is the key duplication nearly impossible because of the lack of tumbler exposure, but there is little room for pick movement within the cylinder. This is the lock's primary defense against picking.

Tension wrench play is important here, but only after the pins have quit clicking into shear line. You will have to support the bottom edge of the Katana with a finger or thumb from your tension wrench hand so that you can rock the pick. Keep the rocking angles low as the pins break fairly shallow as mentioned above. Note that the row of pins that click into shear line first are on the upper left if you are turning right, and vice versa.

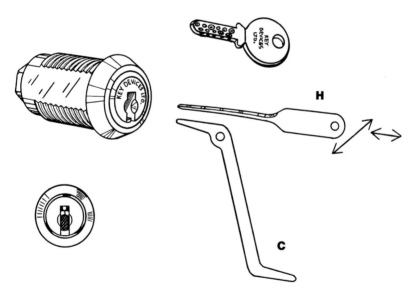

Figure 4C. Picking the three-row pin tumbler Alpha with the Katana ("H") pick. The samurai's direct approach: All pins at once.

Now, if the above technique does not work for the Alpha lock, then try the needle-raking/diamond technique mentioned for the KABA lock below.

Once you have picked this lock, you may wonder if (after you've turned the cylinder 90 degrees) the top driver pins in the shell will snap down and lock the left bottom pins that were riding in the cylinder. That will not happen to this type of lock because the pin rows are staggered and do not line up with their adjacent rows.

Pick resistance: Though I was impressed with the principle and the machining of this lock, the fact that it was full of pins makes it more difficult to pick than it appears. I give it a **7.5,** but this is still very good security as the key is very difficult to duplicate and the lock is time-consuming to pick. Priced around $22 plus $2 key.

Key Devices carries another lock invented by Gallagher—a keyed disc tumbler lock for the gaming industry that can also be used as a cam lock for sliding cabinet doors or an "inner cylinder" for T-handle functions on various types of vending and gaming machines. See Chapter 9 for the analysis of this lock.

THE KABA CAM LOCK

The Swiss-made KABA "Gemini T restricted keyway" also uses a dimple key. This new "stud" pin design was invented by Arno Kleinhaeny of Switzerland in 1995 (U.S. Patent #5,438,857). The Gemini T is an upscaled version of the Alpha Slot Machine Lock, with tighter tolerances and studded pins. Like the Alpha, it has three rows of pins that overlap when engaged by the key, but picking *this* lock is a real exercise in patience.

The lock looks and acts very much like the Alpha. The side pins, like those in the Alpha, come in at an upward angle of about 45 degrees to the horizontal, but have the tips of the pins machined down to a smaller diameter to thwart the use of a Katana-like pick. The top pins are not machined down.

In essence, the edged-pick gets caught on the shoulders of the stud pin's tip. This is what the company means when it refers to their "restricted keyway."

Unlike the Alpha, the KABA cam lock has 16 pins—five on the left, five on top, and six on the right. The vending machine lock or inner cylinder type with the locking-dog catch has 13 pins—five on the left, four on top and four on the right.

The ends of the pins in the Gemini T actually cross each other very closely when aligned, making a straight lock pick of just about any kind useless. If you try to pick the top row of pins and manage to align them, the side row studs must be pushed aside, which puts most of those pins too far into their drivers. So how do you pick this one?

Like all other locks, it has an inherent weakness: the upper left- and right-hand corners allow just enough room for a pin—a straight pin, that is (the next illustration exaggerates these gaps or the width of the keyway). So a different approach is needed when picking this lock.

Let's practice on the KABA 13-pin lock. Since the keyway is rather wide, use the large end of the Tiger tension wrench and apply tension as if you were picking a regular pin tumbler house lock. I found the best pick for this job is a large sewing needle, such as a light-duty carpet needle measuring between .030" to .036" in diameter. Round off the end on a grinder, then file smooth to prevent impaling yourself, but be sure that most of the tip remains. I mounted my needle by heating the eye-end with a lighter and inserting it into a plastic dowel rod. Using the eye of the needle allows the molten plastic to flow into it, which anchors it to the make-shift handle. To avoid ruining the fingerprints on your thumb and forefinger, use pliers to hold the hot needle during heating and insertion.

Next, while applying tension, you want to fully insert the needle pick into the upper left corner of the keyway and use the length of the shaft to push down and right—toward the center of the keyway—as you slowly and gently pull the pick out of the lock. The rounded ends of the stud pins in the left row and pins in the top row will push in—some harder than others—but some of those pins and studs will align. Then go to the right corner and do the same, pulling out and down and to the left. You will feel and hear some of the loose bottom pins rattling within the cylinder while doing this. Because of the shallow breaking of their shear lines, those pins are most likely aligned. Now lightly rock the needle pick directly against the bottom of the top row of pins.

It is doubtful that the cylinder will pop open the first time you do this, so very carefully release tension (sometimes

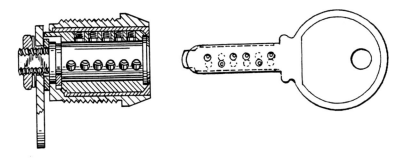

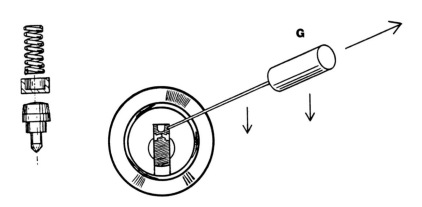

Figure 4D. Raking the three-row, 16-stud pin KABA lock with a needle pick ("G"). The tension wrench is not shown in the illustration.

cylinder locks pop open while releasing the tension wrench) to drop the pins and try again. Sometimes a sideways rocking motion of the pick will pop the lock. I have even tried using a circular motion with the pick. But the three times that I popped this lock, I used the method described above. Be sure that you use tension wrench play while picking.

On the 16-pin KABA lock, I alternated the needle pick with a small diamond. While maintaining tension wrench pressure as before, pick the upper left and top rows simultaneously with the needle pick by stroking the whole needle down, raking both rows. For both the 13- and 16-pin KABA Gemini T, while working the needle, point the tip down as you rake in one, single stroke outward. This will allow the tip to engage each pin in both rows individually as you draw the tip of the needle out of the lock. (This is done because the tips of the tumbler pins and studs intermingle with each other.) Then pull the needle completely out and run the small diamond in as if you were lightly raking a standard pin tumbler lock. Do this once with the diamond, concentrating on the top row only. Second, pull the diamond out and re-insert the needle to rake down the right and top row of pins. Alternate between the two picks (this is where that third hand would be useful); rake upper left and top rows, then small diamond pick top row; rake upper right and top rows, then small diamond top row; then carefully release tension and start over, varying the needle angle each time. While alternating picks, maintain a light tension on the cylinder.

You may also use a Feather Touch tension wrench on this lock if you have trouble opening it. Either Feather Touch wrench will fit into this keyway, however, with so many pins, and since there are no spool or mushroom pins, you may want the direct contact of the cylinder with your fingers through a stiffer wrench so that you can better feel the pins.

Pick resistance: This lock is very time-consuming. The quality and machining of this mechanism makes picking this lock a daunting task for the inexperienced locksmith. I found this lock to be tough to pick and rated it at **8.0**.

Topless Chisel Pin Side-Bar Locks

So just how do you make a pick-resistant pin tumbler lock with no top pins? Maybe we should look to how this species evolved: Remember the side-bar flat wafer tumbler locks used on GM autos since 1935?[1] Medeco turned those flat wafers into round, chisel-pointed pins with grooves and holes in the sides to align with a sidebar. Waitress! My tab, please! So here, "topless" does *not* mean that we are at first base.

Here, the real action is with the pin in the bottom—which has direct contact with the key. But before we can understand how a topless pin tumbler lock could be effective security, we must first examine the basic principle established by Medeco—the originator of the rotating chisel pin.

TWISTED TUMBLERS

Medeco locks have been around since 1970, though the first U.S. patent (#3,722,240) wasn't issued until March 1973.

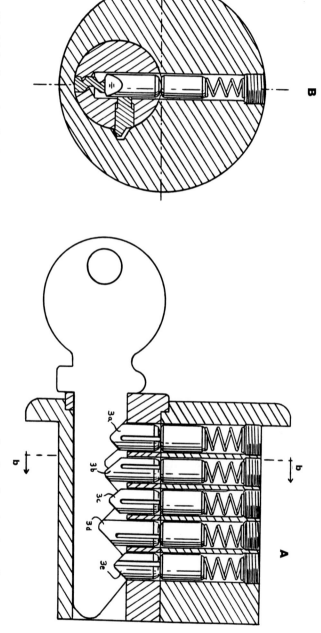

Figure 5A. Medeco's rotating chisel pin tumbler principle. Note that the vertical groove in each chisel pin must align with the side-bar as well as break with the cylinder before the lock can be opened.

Now owned by the ASSA/Abloy Group, no single lock company has had such an impact on modern security. The rotating pin or "twisting tumbler" concept patented (#4,635,455) by inventor Roy N. Oliver for Medeco Security Locks was designed to increase the number of key changes, thus improving security. In the process, he also created a more pick-resistant lock, as each tumbler must be positioned exactly for its groove (or hole) to align with the lock's side-bar rails or posts. Moreover, the chiseled pointed pins can rotate either forward or in reverse by up to 20 degrees on each side, with either left- or right-handed pins. See Figure 5B to view the skewed cuts on the key control where these pins align their slots (Figure 5B, #4) with the side-bar in addition to the standard rising of the pins to a breaking shear line with the cylinder. The tang (Figure 5B, #1) on each pin rides a broached slot[2] in the pin chamber of the plug and limits total rotation or spin of each tumbler in each direction (forward or reverse) by 20 degrees. The key (Figure 5A, item c) can be cut skewed by either 10 or 20 degrees in either direction or straight across perpendicular with the bit in any variation on the blank. Here, a key is shown with six cuts for a six-pin Medeco lock. As of this printing, this is the highest number of pins any Medeco may have.

For ease of manufacturing, there are only five distinctly different chisel points in a Medeco lock (refer to Figure 5A, item a):

- rear offset long chisel face (shown as item 3d in Figure 5A and item d in Figure 5B)
- rear offset short (item 3e)
- forward offset long (3b and item i in Figure 5B)
- forward offset short (3a)
- centered or no-offset chisel pin (3c)

The skewed key cuts can be either centered, skewed left 10 or 20 degrees, or skewed right 10 or 20 degrees. This gives the manufacturer 10 distinctly different types of tumblers to

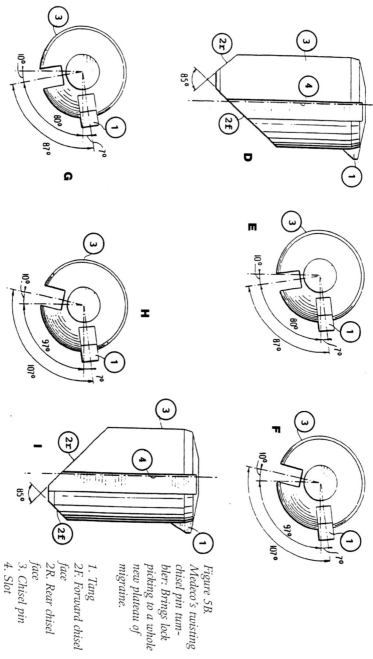

Figure 5B.
Medeco's twisting
chisel pin tum-
bler: Brings lock
picking to a whole
new plateau of
migraine.

1. Tang
2F. Forward chisel
face
2R. Rear chisel
face
3. Chisel pin
4. Slot

use in each lock, along with the centered chisel tumbler with a .030" bias either in front or to the rear of centerline, making 13 distinct tumblers. This adds immense variety to the key code for each lock.

Referring back to Figure 5A, item c—at the top edge view of the Medeco key we see the extent to which these tumblers may twist before they can align with side-bar and shear line. Here, don't be concerned with the exact key and tumbler dimensions when picking this or any other pin tumbler lock; feel and visualization are the best guides. This patent, #4,635,455, will expire Jan. 13, 2007, but the race for better security will undoubtedly continue.

THE MEDECO THREE-PIN ALARM SWITCH LOCK

With only three pin tumblers, this little bombshell is packed with finely machined parts. Invented by Stevie C. Roop for Medeco back in 1989 (U.S. Patent #4,829,798), it has dual function—both as a switch lock and cam lock. But don't let the low number of pins fool you. Like its Daddy, the six-pin Medeco door lock (next chapter), it has a side-bar, but only has one spool pin (could be any tumbler.) Again, note that there are no top pins. The pin's flattened, chiseled ends also helps to prevent a rogue key from entering the keyway. But the Monkey pick ("K") can go right past the bouncer at the door— without paying the cover charge—and play with the pins. This is because the Monkey pick is much thinner and smaller than the key and can rotate the pins by its raking motion.

Once the pin has been turned (and it can turn a maximum of only 20 degrees in either direction) it can be raised and the groove (or hole in some Medecos) in its side can align with the side bar rails (or posts). But this alignment cannot occur until each pin has been raised to the right height as well. So once you have freed each pin by a slight rotation, you then have to position each pin vertically to clear cylinder shear line and so that the side bar will align and retract by the force of turning the cylinder. And this is where the Monkey comes in.

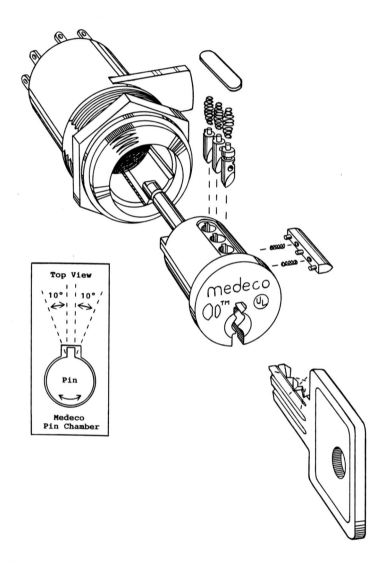

Figure 5C. Tougher than it looks: an exploded view of the Medeco three-pin tumbler, combination switch/cam lock.

Here's how to pick these little jewels: Approach the lock as if it were an automobile wafer side-bar, but use the standard Monkey pick (formerly the "twisted wedge-point," but ground on both sides instead of bent for smoother action) with a White Crane Feather Touch tension wrench. Gently run the pick in and out of the keyway while very lightly applying torque to the Feather Touch wrench. The wrench pressure can be no greater than the tension of the side-bar springs, but it must also be great enough to compress the side bar should the tumblers align with it, if you can imagine that. These side bar springs have very low force, so keep your torque light. Once the cylinder pops, you'll need to choke up (slide your grip up toward the lock face) on the Crane wrench and turn the cylinder by the Crane's head for the force needed to unlatch the cam or lower the dog (on T-handle locks). Be careful when the cylinder pops as the Crane has the tendency to fly out of the keyway, allowing the cylinder to snap back and re-lock itself.

Pick resistance: This is a good alarm switch lock—better than what has predominated the market in the past—but the three pins make it relatively easy to open for this category of lock. Still, I rated at a healthy **8.5**.

THE MEDECO FOUR-PIN POP LOCK

This lock, holding the new type of chisel pin invented by Roop (U.S. Patent #4,829,798), is a small marvel in engineering and is tough to pick. The topless pins, like that of the above lock but with one more pin, also ride a vertical groove and must align the hole in their side with the side-bar posts. Having an extra pin seems to make a big difference (as these locks take a while to pick) but sometimes you can get lucky and pop one in 20 minutes. Follow the procedure described on the last lock above. So far I have picked this one four times (the last time took me longer than the first time). The point here is that these types of locks require time as well as skill to open.

The majority of the skill needed here is with the tension

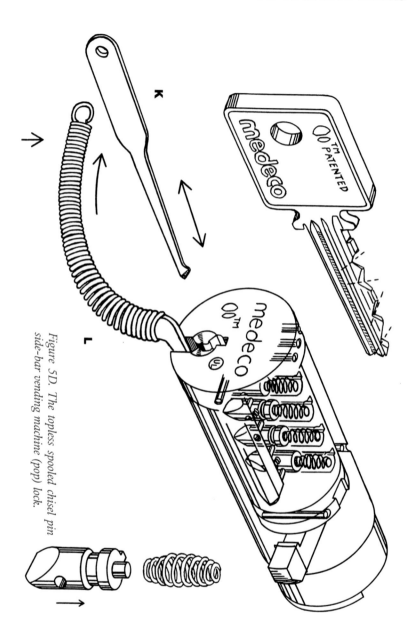

Figure 5D. The topless spooled chisel pin side-bar vending machine (pop) lock.

wrench, not the pick, though some skill is needed there as well. It's essential that you learn to use both hands independently of each other—to work both halves of the brain. This is the key to opening topless spooled pin side-bar locks.

While picking the locks in this chapter, you will frequently snag a pin. This occurs when the top of the pin's horizontal spool groove engages the leading edge of the cylinder due to its torque. You'll know when this happens if the cylinder gives a little to the right and stops after only a few degrees (usually, these locks open clockwise). When this happens, stop picking. Release the tension wrench until all the pins drop back down and start the picking all over again. There is no further need to keep picking, as the cylinder can't turn while that pin is snagged.

If this happens, you are trying too hard. Try using less upward motion of the pick and remember to keep the torque light. My White Crane tension wrench pressure varies from about 45 to 90 degrees in an arc. This data is dependent on the spring that you may have used for your Crane wrench.[3]

The keyway of this lock is designed to foil the setting or fixing of the tension wrench on the cylinder. Near the bottom of the keyway are two ridges that run across from each other and restrict the entrance of foreign objects. The White Crane tension wrench is designed to enter and affix itself to this and similar keyways. I have tried picking this lock with a looped Feather Touch ("M") wrench[4]—the kind sold in locksmith supply companies—but while it has a good feel for the pins, there is little room for the pick. This is important, as the act of raking the chisel-pointed pins causes them to rotate to their proper positions.

Occasionally pull on the end of the Crane wrench spring to stretch it. This is for tension variation, but be sure to maintain an overall light clockwise force. After spending about an hour trying to pick my sample lock the first time, it popped open. Light tension wrench pressure did it—just as I was about to pull out the tools to give up. Also, if you have trouble with your sample lock, try using a small diamond pick

("B") instead of the Monkey, as a pin might have to break low in your cylinder.

Pick resistance: This stainless steel lock is tough. Not only is it tough to pick, but it's made to withstand a bullet. In fact, a bullet would just piss it off, as the mechanism is so finely machined that any unreasonable force may flatten the side-bar alignment pins and jam the cylinder up tight. It is also loaded with three hardened anti-drill pins running vertically and one in the side of the face, along with two anti-pull pins near the back of the lock. See illustration. This is good security so I rated it at a healthy **10.0**.

THE MEDECO DURACAM GAMING MACHINE LOCK

When I first saw this lock in one of my locksmith's catalogs, I had to have it. Any lock that looked like "Pac Man" from the video game tables of the early 1980s had to be interesting. Looking down this keyway, one can see that there is plenty of room in there. Reminds me of a bowling alley.

This unique "horizontal keyway" design (U.S. Patent #4,635,455)[5] is more to prevent unauthorized key duplication (one of the biggest headaches in gaming) than to prevent picking—though this lock does that, too. The wide keyway is to allow for a thicker key, as broken-off keys in the locks are the second biggest headache in the gaming business when it comes to gaming machine locks.

Note how the key is cut at different angles across the flat side, rather than on the edge of the key as in the above locks. The key is cut deeply into its corrugated face. This means that the pins break low in the keyway, making little room for most lock picks. That is the only difference between this lock and the above locks in this chapter. This, too, is a side-bar mechanism that requires pretty much the same treatment as the four-pin pop lock above. The chisel pins must be jostled into place while the cylinder taps at the side-bar.

But in this case, because of the keyway design, we use dif-

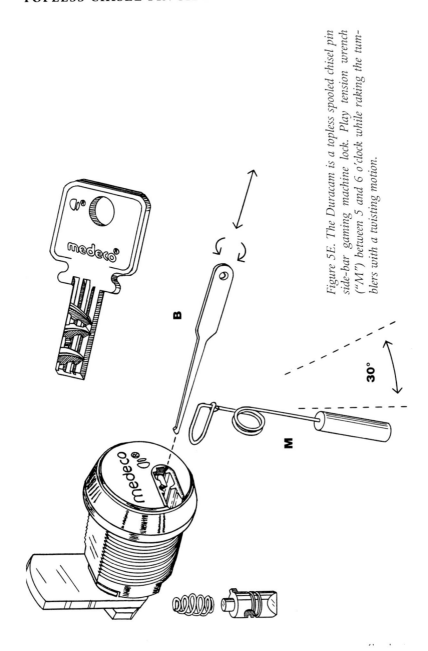

Figure 5E. The Duracam is a topless spooled chisel pin side-bar gaming machine lock. Play tension wrench ("M") between 5 and 6 o'clock while raking the tumblers with a twisting motion.

ferent tools and technique. You'll need to run a small diamond pick through the keyway with its back seated along the lower right-hand corner of the keyway. In Figure 5E you may view the pick top-edge-on as you slip it into the lock. (Also, all picks in the illustrations of this book are shown not burnished for detail. You must burnish your picks before using them or they will file off shavings from the tumblers and keyway and hinder picking.) You then want to give the pick an intermittent twist while inserting and withdrawing in order to rotate and push the tumblers up into place. In essence, you are using the side edge of your small diamond pick to raise the tumblers with the twisting.

The trick is to get a Feather Touch wrench seated in the keyway. Here is where the classic looped Feather Touch is of good use. The lock illustrated was set up for a counterclockwise turn by simply reversing the cam stop at the rear of the lock. This was the best way to show how the wrench would go into, and travel across, the lock. It inserts with its handle hanging down to the 6:30 position. When the proper force is applied, the wrench handle would point to the 5 o'clock position. While running the pick in and out with a twisting motion, vary the tension wrench pressure between 5 and 6 o'clock to set up the best transient conditions needed for the pins to align with the side-bar.

The easiest way to get the feel for this lock is to take it apart. First, simply take the cam lock cylinder out of its shell by removing the rear holding nut, cam, and cam stop. The cylinder with all its springs, pins, and side-bar will stay together, as it is self-contained. But the advantage for the locksmith here is that the keyway is exposed along the cylinder's length so that you can see and manipulate the pins while you press down on the side-bar with your finger.

Now, the uniqueness that makes side-bar locks difficult to pick is that from the outside at the face of the lock, you cannot apply direct pressure onto the side-bar to make the pins click into place. Being within a shell, the cylinder cannot turn until the side-bar is forced into place by the turning of the proper key. And this cannot happen until all the pins are aligned first.

But in this case, by applying direct pressure on the side-bar with a finger, one can see and feel each pin clicking into place, causing the side-bar to drop down flush with the cylinder. Sometimes, while picking the exposed cylinder this way, the side-bar will drop on one corner, then the other. Also, one can see when you snag a pin as the side-bar goes down only about halfway—not enough to clear the inner wall of the shell.

When picking this lock, be sure that the bottom edge of your small diamond pick runs down the very back of the key-way, or "Pac Man's" mouth. Turn the pick slightly clockwise as you run it in and out of the keyway. It takes a while to develop a feel for this way of picking; the tip of your pick will engage the tumblers sideways, so you will be using the side of the tool. Because of this, I find this lock almost fun to pick.

Pick resistance: This lock is made more for durability with key use than it is for pick resistance. But the wide key-way allows for plenty of room to manipulate the pins. I rated it at a **10.0** (includes one extra half point for originality, as most burglars would not know where to start with this strange-looking lock). It still took me more than 60 minutes to open this lock my first time.

1. *Secrets of Lock Picking*, Paladin Press, pp. 23-26
2. A broached slot is an internal slot that runs the vertical length of the pin chamber through both the lock shell and cylinder.
3. Please refer back to Chapter 1 for the spring dynamics of this wrench. This spring is specifically chosen for our tension wrench because of its characteristics.
4. *Secrets of Lock Picking*, Paladin Press, p. 9, figure 5D. Further research on my part has revealed that this tool is no longer available in locksmith's supply chains. Please see Chapter 1 for details in making this tool.
5. Note the identical patent numbers between the "Pop Lock" and the "Duracam" locks. This told me before I even started working with these two locks that they operate on the same principle. However, the Duracam is covered by the above patent because of the "claim" or "claims" detailing its unique keyway, which is perpendicular (right angle) to the action of the pins and horizontal keyway. This is the only true difference between the two locks. For more about patents and claims, see *Patent Secrets* by Steven Hampton and Craig Herrington.

Mushroom
Chisel Pin
Side-Bar Locks

Modern high-security locks have not evolved in an order-ly, calm, progressive sequence. Sometimes evolutionary steps are skipped because of the ingenuity and marketing skills of the inventors of such systems. Some great ideas fall away; an incredible lock may come along only to be waysided by lack of knowledge on what to do next or just because of bad luck.[1] But most new, modern locks are sophisticated hybrids that are on the drawing boards of the big companies such as Medeco and the ASSA/Abloy Group.[2] The latter, by the way, has recently bought out the Yale Lock Co., one of the old schools of security—and locksmithing, for that matter. A new era in locksmithing has taken root.

What this all means is that there will be more high-secu-rity locking systems to come. Only large companies will be equipped to tool up for and maintain these well-organized keying systems for their customers. Duplicate keys will have to be ordered from the lock maker through the locksmith, making copying a key quickly impossible. Also, each key made will be logged into the lock maker's database, making unauthorized copies less likely. (You won't be able to take your boss's key down to the local lock shop for a personal copy on your lunch break. Aside from the embarrassment, your boss would get a phone call.)

Actually, we have been discussing these restricted locks, which have special keying requirements, since Chapter 4 (the Van lock and on . . .)

Now, the security steps up to an even more intense stage. If a species is to survive, it adapts and changes, carrying along with it all the genetic benefits of its past generations. In the same way, the pin tumbler lock has adapted to its environment and has evolved to the next level. It shows no signs of going extinct. This next group of locks is here to stay.

THE MEDECO FOUR-PIN PAYPHONE LOCK

In the last classification of pin tumbler locks (in the previous chapter) we discussed the use of chisel-pointed rotating pins, but it is within this classification that such a rotating pin has more impact, the reason being that these locks have top pins. But not just top pins; one or more of them can be a mushroom pin. And like the mushrooms growing in your yard as a child—the ones that mother told you not to eat—this mushroom can cause severe acid indigestion.

Because of these top pins the bottom pins can rotate more freely, as the tumbler springs are not pushing directly down on the chisel pins. This makes the pins a little more slippery when it comes to raking the lock.

If you are a thief and happen to be reading this, you may have assumed by the above subtitle of this chapter and lock type that you would never have to pay for a phone call again; but this is not why I included this lock in this chapter. I did so because this lock is coming into common use today and it is a unique and tough lock to pick. Also, many of these locks are used on privately owned pay phones—phones owned by individuals—and again, my intention is not to cause others loss. But because of the difficulty involved in picking this lock, I seriously doubt if this chapter will cause its extinction. Let's have some fun and tackle this one together.

Medeco, once again, has come up with a uniquely different and difficult to pick key-operated mechanism for the consumer, albeit a combination of past systems. Note the anti-drill pins in its face. Behind them are anti-punch and pull plates (the half-moon shaped discs). If a thief were to drill into this lock, he would get to break his drill bit. The next morning, the locksmith would get to carefully file out the keyway so that the owner's key would slip into the lock so that it could be opened and replaced—with coin box intact. But for the thief, the drill pins and punch plates are just the tip of the iceberg when it comes to breaking into this lock.

The bottom pins in this lock have more grooves than an old hippie reunion. These grooves are arranged in a vertical (up and down) and horizontal (left to right) fashion. The deep vertical groove must align with the studs on the back of the side-bar so that it can retract when the cylinder is turned. This groove is a deep V-shaped slot along the length of the pin (see blow-up of the bottom pin in the drawing) and its placement varies. The shallow vertical grooves are "fake" to confuse the expert lock picker; the side-bar will give a little when it encounters these grooves, and its compression locks up the pins from further rotary movement. The pin will still elevate, however, this pin lock-up prevents a rogue key from entering. Because the chiseled pin can't rotate, it leads the lock picker to believe that he is still picking the lock and that the pin is aligned.

The horizontal grooves act as shallow spool pins, which is another picking deterrent—a job normally associated with top (driver) pins.

The top pins in this lock are smooth, except for the mushroom driver(s), naturally, but these top pins do not have much area to engage shear line. So spooling them would require a larger diameter cylinder—which isn't necessary. Along with its tight, corrugated keyway this lock is damn near pick-proof.

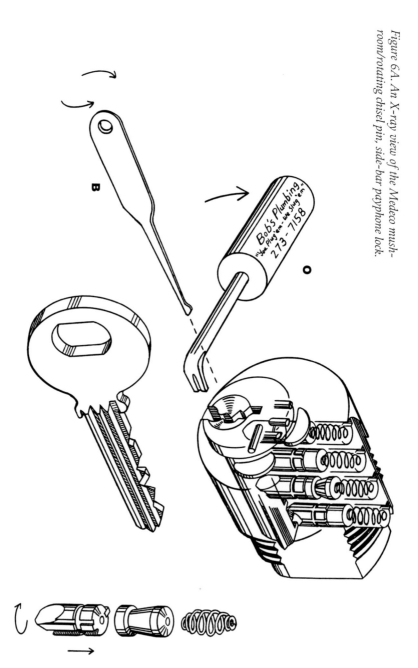

B

Bob's Plumbing
"You Plug 'em - we Slug 'em"
273 - 7158

All-in-all, this lock is well designed in that nearly all the possible ways to secure the cylinder seem to have been utilized.

In Figure 6A, note the tiny spring behind the side-bar and seated between the side-bar's rails. This is one of two springs that maintain an outward force on the side-bar to keep it in the locked position. Generally, a side-bar also helps to resist the forced turning of the cylinder.

I first tried picking this lock using the White Crane tension wrench with a twisting force at its very end. I mounted the wrench into the bottom of the keyway upside down—that's right, upside down Crane. (Refer to Figure 7F.) This creates a uniform force along the length of the cylinder. When done properly, it will loop around the top face of the lock while you are doing this, to the right of the lock face when turning right, and vice versa the other direction. But, there is still room to slide the pick in.

The pick best for this job is the small diamond, no more than .031″ thick. Even though the keyway is tight, this pick can maneuver quite easily along its length to engage the pins. (The standard Monkey pick will not fit into this keyway with a tension wrench inserted.) Use a gentle, raking motion while occasionally rocking the pick up and down slightly (this will be sufficient to rotate the pins while they are being elevated). Do this to get a feel for the lock. Vary the motions each time you pick to try all the options that are available with these tools.

The first time I popped this lock in this fashion, my Crane flew the coop and the cylinder snapped back tight. So, if you have trouble with this technique, try the looped Feather Touch wrench. There was less room for the pick, but I managed to open it again. This wrench will also help you find just which driver pin(s) are mushroomed, as this type of Feather Touch wrench has a slightly stiffer torque.

Sometimes, on certain locks like this one, you need a stiff wrench to find the mushroom pin(s). Because this keyway has a wide opening at its bottom, I discovered that the TuBar tension wrench fits nicely into this shallow part of the opening.

This allowed me to get a firm grip (but still, with a light touch) on the cylinder so as to find the mushroom pin causing all the problems. I then went back to using the looped wrench, and remembering where this pin was, I raised it slightly higher than the other pins to clear the mushroom "cap" pin end.

Because the side-bar spring pressure is so high in this lock, a stiff tension wrench is needed to compress it to turn the cylinder when you do get the pins aligned. However, if too much tension wrench torque is applied, then the mushroom pin(s) snags the cylinder. So one must alternate between wrenches to get a feel for that particular lock. As always with spooled and mushroom pins, if the cylinder seems eager to turn but won't, then you probably snagged one of them and must release tension to start over again.

Pick resistance: This lock is excellent security. The engineering of the bottom pins is a marvel of machining. Setting up to manufacture these pins for production—with several different pin configurations—must have been a huge challenge. The first pick took me 97 minutes, the second, about 38 minutes. But, oddly, I haven't been able to pick this lock open a third time so I rated this lock high: A respectable **11.0**.

THE MEDECO SIX-PIN DOOR LOCK

This Medeco lock has been around for some time now and has proven to be an effective deterrent to picking. As we have seen, Medeco locks use a rotating bottom chisel pin. Again, it is not that the chisel pin has to rotate to clear at the shear line, rather, it has to turn to allow the side-bar's rails to align with the pin's grooves.

The key is cut to turn the pins as it enters the keyway. So a rogue key—or even another Medeco key—cannot enter the cylinder, as the pins will jam up when turning the cylinder. But this is not what makes most Medeco locks so difficult to pick open; it's the fine machining of the lock itself.

Note in Figure 6B the following items: #6 marks the anti-pull/punch plates and #5 marks the anti-drill pins. These are

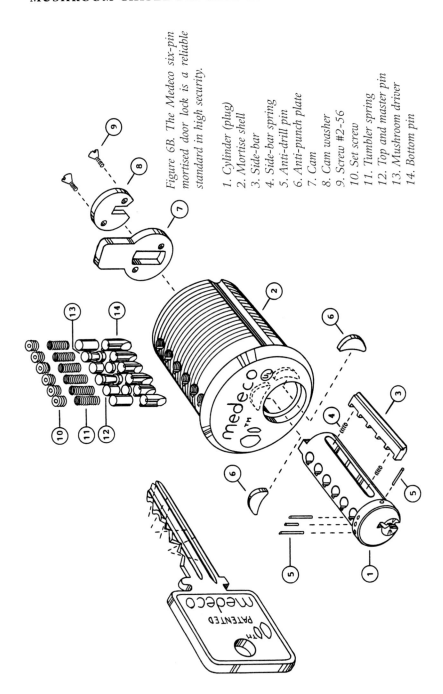

Figure 6B. The Medeco six-pin mortised door lock is a reliable standard in high security.

1. Cylinder (plug)
2. Mortise shell
3. Side-bar
4. Side-bar spring
5. Anti-drill pin
6. Anti-punch plate
7. Cam
8. Cam washer
9. Screw #2-56
10. Set screw
11. Tumbler spring
12. Top and master pin
13. Mushroom driver
14. Bottom pin

relatively new additions to the security features of these locks, along with Roy Oliver's patented pins. The older Medeco mortise cylinders did not use anti-drill pins and anti-pull/punch plates. About 25 years ago (in the mid-1970s), Medeco started using an anti-drill pin in the face of their cylinders. Over the years, they increased the anti-drill pins and added the anti-pull/punch plates as well and the Medeco 10 series mortise cylinder lock is the result.

But, the only real difference in the 10 series mortise cylinder from the four-pin phone lock is the two extra pins and the lack of horizontal grooves on the bottom pins. You can pick this lock much like the four-pin phone lock above. But this keyway has room for the Monkey pick, if you prefer. I found that there is also room for the looped Feather Touch wrench as well and since there are no horizontal grooves across the bottom pins, this makes up the difference for the two extra pins. In essence, the two locks are nearly equal in security.

Pick resistance: In *Secrets of Lock Picking*, I mentioned that I picked this lock once many years ago. But leaving nostalgia behind, in reality, this time it seemed much tougher—around 110 minutes—probably because of Oliver's chisel pins. I also believe that the overall machining has improved. I would have to rate this lock at **11.5**.

1. Conceiving, developing, and prototyping an invention is one thing. Getting it profitably to market without someone stealing it is another. For more information on inventions and inventing, see author's other work, *Patent Secrets*, Paladin Press.

2. As of the year 2000, Medeco was also acquired by the ASSA/Abloy Group.

7

Spooled/Mushroom Multiple Row Side-Bar Locks

Just when you think you have mastered the pin tumbler and all of its descendants—when you know you are the expert and the party is really rocking—a turd surfaces in the punch bowl. This is how the next lock group hit me. But, like an old friend and kung fu master once said, "This isn't heaven—this is the human realm."[1]

And this class of locks "isn't heaven" for a good reason. Take the best six-pin tumbler lock you have ever encountered and throw a five-pin tumbler GM side-bar into the works for good measure. Now, make sure all of those pins align at the same time before you even try to turn the cylinder with your tension wrench. See the problem? Not enough hands.

THE RUKO EUROPEAN BANK DOOR LOCK

Single row pin tumbler locks are relatively easy to pick, even if a spool or mushroom pin is thrown in for kicks; with a little bit of patience and skill, one can pop a six-pin within a reasonable amount of time. But what happens when you are presented with another row of pins out of symmetry with the main row? An Alpha or even a KABA can be picked without having to bring your lunch because the three rows of pins are arranged close together—and the pick can be utilized in one area within the keywell.

But when the rows are separated by the height of the keyway, one begins to ponder if it would not be easier to sprout an extra hand out of one's bellybutton.

Such is the Danish-made Ruko, a high-security lock that has a cylinder that sports 11 pins—six standard pins at center top and a five-pin side-bar down to the lower left side of the cylinder.[2] Amazingly, this lock has been in use for more than 20 years.

If, as an American, you should ever encounter this lock, chances are you are in the old country visiting neighborhood tourist shoppes. (However, we wouldn't want someone to use this information to rip off our European neighbors and friends. It would take so long to pick this lock that someone would turn the thief in to the local police, and being arrested in a foreign country with lock picks would ruin the vacation—indefinitely.) A few decades ago, this lock graced bank doors in various parts of Europe. But it is wise not to be too curious of locked doors in foreign countries unless you are specifically trained to be a spook. This lock is out of production, as Ruko is no longer in business. ASSA makes the IC (also known as replacement cylinders) for the Ruko locks still in use.

Note how the key is cut as if it were two keys in one. Also note the small steel rod embedded in both sides of the keyway entrance. This effectively deters drilling the brass cylinder by snagging the drill bit. Behind the cylinder face is a hardened anti-drill plate that catches the drill bit tip (should it break through the face) and takes the whole drill for a merry-go-round ride in the burglar's hands.

Also note that all of the six top pins in the main row are spooled. The five side-bar pins, though not spooled, offer an

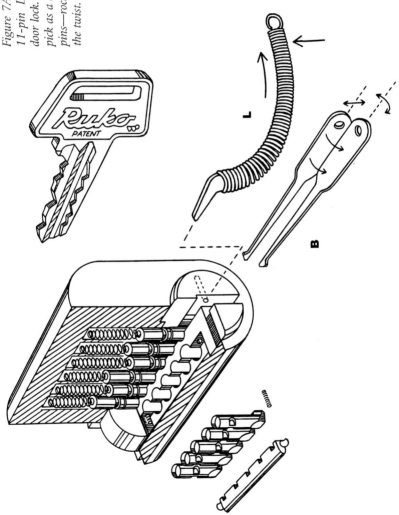

Figure 7A. Cutaway view of the 11-pin Danish-made Ruko IC door lock. Use the small diamond pick as a dual-function rake: Top pins—rock and roll. Side pins—the twist.

even bigger challenge in that they are chiseled—and unlike what we learned in the last chapter, these pins do not rotate. Instead, they are chiseled to allow for the very tip of the pin to catch as much of the key cuts (on the left lower side of the key) as possible because these cuts have little surface area to interface with the pins. In fact, the side-bar pins have a little tab near their ends so as to engage the lower key cuts more completely.

Also, the side-bar pins are "pinched" on their sides and these indentations (which are actually machined into the pin sides) align in vertical fashion with the side-bar slots to allow the side-bar to retract and release the cylinder. The tops of these pins are recessed into a bowl-like depression to seat and retain the end of a spring, unlike the side-bar pins in the top-less spool pin locks that we discussed that use a peg to center and hold the spring. This minor difference, however, does not affect the way the lock functions, or is picked.

When picking the Ruko cylinder, use a small diamond pick (with a thickness of no more than .025" as the keyway is fairly corrugated) and a Feather Touch wrench. The looped wrench has a good tension and feel, but the Crane (with its .035" thick end) fits the keyway the best as it has a lower end-profile.

Place the tip of the Crane tension wrench at the top of the keyway (center of the cylinder face) so that you have room to run the pick in and out. Also, so the whole lock could be shown, Figure 7A depicts the Crane tension wrench positioned right side up. You want to mount the wrench upside down—the key-chain end of the wrench will loop over the top half of the lock. This is so you have room to maneuver the small diamond pick within the keywell. (Refer to Figure 7F.)

First, rake the six main tumblers on center line as you would any good spooled-pin tumbler lock. Rake the pins until they feel like you have moved them into some kind of position for alignment; do not rake until you snag a spool pin, as this will defeat the purpose of even going on with the next part of this procedure.

Next, while maintaining wrench pressure, pull out the

pick and turn the same small diamond pick to the 90 degrees horizontal left—a "lazy diamond"—and slide the pick down to the lower left of the keyway. Now, rake this lower left set of five pins with a subtle twist of the pick. Do not teeter the pick. Gently twist it, but not too much—there is little clearance at the base of these side-bar pins and their tabs to the bottom of the keyway. Here, you don't have to worry about snagging a pin as these pins are not spooled and do not rotate.

You must alternate between these two sets of pins until the cylinder gives way to top pin snagging. Once snagged, release the cylinder of tension and drop the pins back down to start over. This type of tension wrench play is an important factor while picking high-security locks. The skilled lock picker will recognize the moment such treatment is needed on the lock when the cylinder engages the pick (via the tumblers) and responds directly to the motion of the tension wrench.

Pick resistance: Committed to picking this lock, I was Shanghied by my own ego onto a banana-boat cruise of frustration, and after two weeks of picking (I lost count of how many hours I had logged on this whacked-out tour of duty) I awoke with a drunkard's head. My bloodshot eyes fell upon my hands as they trembled the tools within the whored cylinder. I blinked. That moment, she slipped effortlessly open to port.

"I am free!" I cracked with hoarse voice as the shackles of pick and wrench fell from my joint-aching fingers. "FREE!" I exclaimed with clearing throat as the tools plinked into the submerging deck at my feet. They floated down like lost silver coins, resting flat and gleaming back at the sun-lighted hatch above my louse-ridden head.

Anyway, that's the way it felt when I finally popped this ball 'n' chain. But now, as I write this, I wonder if I didn't open it because I wore the pins down from sheer repetition and countless snagging of the spools. (I am certain though, that at the very least, the keyway is wider.) Actually, I exaggerate here—this lock is stainless steel. But, I haven't been able to (or felt the desire to) walk that plank again. Arrrrrr! This is a very high-security lock. I give the Ruko 11-pin tumbler/side-bar a pick resistant value of **12**.

And if that doesn't discourage the enterprising pirate, Ruko came up with a spooled, multi-pin row, multi side-bar lock (the Twintronic) that also incorporates an electronic recognition system within the cylinder and key. We will cover this lock in Chapter 10.

THE ASSA 6000—U.S. POST OFFICE DOOR LOCK

Building upon the success of the Ruko, the ASSA 6000 series also features a "coded" side-bar system, making the picking of this lock a supreme challenge. The side pins in the 6000 are all made the same—with two false shallow grooves flanking a deep middle groove—while the side-bar is cut to a code that matches the cuts in the side of the proper key.

The older ASSA 6000 series ICs (U.S. Patents #4,356,713; #4,393,673; #4,577,479) do not spool all of their top pins, but this lock is still, most certainly, considered "high security."

The 6000 comes in a variety of cylinder replacements. You may encounter a Schlage cylinder using this 11-pin set-up and not know it, unless you happen to notice the slightly wider opening at the bottom left of the keyway. These older ASSA 6000 cylinders were considered *the* security lock for the past 17 years and were used on the doors of some U.S. Post Offices (along with another brand lock, the Schlage Primus, which functions on the same principle of the 6000, but with fewer pins. Its patent number is also unpublished). Some post offices still use the 6000. Since the patent recently ran out (U.S. patents issued today are now good for 20 years—upped from 17 years), ASSA has designed the Twin V-10 with a "unique-but-secure keying system, making key duplication—by key machine or by hand—virtually impossible."

The ASSA 6000 ICs being deployed within other brand-name locks now have the insignia "ASSA" on the face of the replacement cylinder. So if you approach one of these cylin-

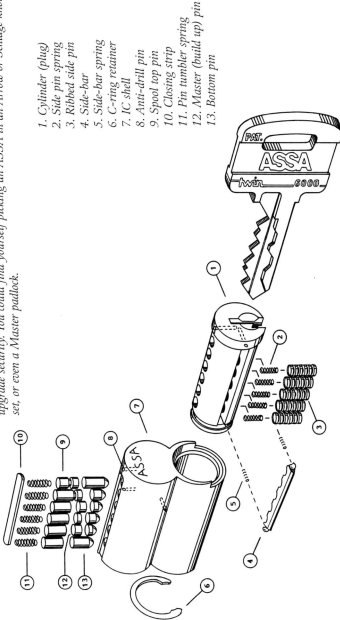

Figure 7B. ASSA's Twin 6000 series cylinders are used in other brand-name locks to upgrade security. You could find yourself picking an ASSA in an Arrow or Schlage knob-set, or even a Master padlock.

1. Cylinder (plug)
2. Side pin spring
3. Ribbed side pin
4. Side-bar
5. Side-bar spring
6. C-ring retainer
7. IC shell
8. Anti-drill pin
9. Spool top pin
10. Closing strip
11. Pin tumbler spring
12. Master (build up) pin
13. Bottom pin

ders, you'll know right away what you are up against.

Other lock companies using the new ASSA system are Arrow, Corbin/Russwin (the companies are now merged), Sargent, and Yale, which now belongs to The ASSA/Abloy Group.

Now, what is bad news for the lock picker is that the upper driver pins in the IC locks are usually spooled—the first, third, and fifth top driver pins at the very least—depending on the locksmith who set up the cylinder. But the worst news is that the lower left pins are side-barred as well.

Pick resistance: This whole group of locks is tough to classify on a scale, but I rated the ASSA 6000 series in general to be very good locks at **12.0.**

ASSA TWIN V-10

In 1999, the patent ran out for the Swedish-made ASSA's Twin 6000 series lock. In order to improve the security of its cylinder, the ASSA Twin V-10 was created (covered by U.S. and Canadian patents #5,067,335 and #5,640,865). Like the Ruko, it has a cylinder that carries 11 pins—six standard pins at center top (but all mushroomed top pins) and a side-bar down to the lower-left side of the cylinder with five more "ribbed side pins" that are heavily spooled. Mushroom top pins are seldom used in other locks, as they can jam up in sloppy cylinders. Here there is little slop, which makes picking very tough.

The side-bar is also very different here. The side-bars are counter-spooled (each lock differently) by their recessed side-pin spaces to make picking even more distasteful. Note how this key is also cut as if it were two keys in one.

The ASSA Twin V-10 is one of the few locks that conforms to U.S. military standards in quality and function. It is listed under Underwriter's Laboratory's test #437, which has been established for high-security locks to determine the cylinder's physical resistance against various forms of attack. It is stainless steel throughout, including the pins (with the exception of case-hardened anti-drill inserts), making this

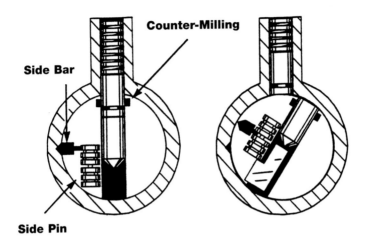

Figure 7C. Frontal cutaway view of the ASSA V10: Making the most out of spool pins.

lock one tuff hombre.

Let me quote from the locksmith's service manual on this gem:

"Inactive 'dummy' grooves in the side pins catch the side bar when improperly positioned. When rotational force is applied to pick this lock, the mushroom-spooled pin tumblers, close tolerances, and counter-milled pin chambers protect the cylinder from virtually every known picking method."[3]

The side pin used in the ASSA Twin V-10 cylinder has four false grooves to confuse picking attempts. Out of five grooves only one, located in one of five positions around the side pin, is deep enough to allow alignment with the side-bar.

Note how the top driver pins in the main central row are not only spooled, *they are mushroomed as well*. The bottom ends of these spooled pins are turned down to a smaller diameter than the rest of the pin barrel, and then rounded on the ends—shaped like a cone-headed mushroom. This enhances their effective pick-resistance value. Plus, the pin chamber counter-milling latches the spools up tight if not raised to

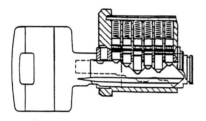 

Figure 7D. Left: A cutaway side view of the ASSA Twin V-10. High precision in a small package—32 moving parts controlled by a key. Right: A peek down the throat of the V-10 cylinder.

their proper height.

The ASSA Twin V-10 has two different ribbed side pins: a left-hand and a right-hand. Like the Ruko, this side pin has a tab for maximum contact with the key cuts along the side of the key. Most locks use the left-hand side pins as is depicted in Figure 7F with the tabs protruding out to the right of the observer. Right-handed side-pin ASSA V-10s can be special-ordered, which messes up any picking skill that one may have mastered while learning the left-hand side-bar arrangement.

ASSA keeps fastidious records on who has what key for each and every one of its locks. You should have heard the discussion that I had while ordering one of these locks; I've applied for loans with less grilling. This company keeps detailed track of every key they make for each and every one of their locks. This shows responsibility on the part of the lock maker and

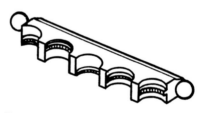

Figure 7E. The ASSA V-10 side-bars: counter-spooled and coded, this finely machined part is designed to catch the ribbed side pins the wrong way while picking.

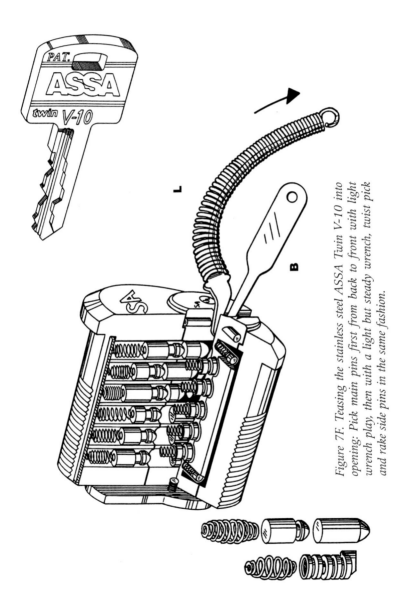

Figure 7F: Teasing the stainless steel ASSA Twin V-10 into opening: Pick main pins first from back to front with light wrench play, then with a light but steady wrench, twist pick and rake side pins in the same fashion.

reflects how security has evolved—if you need a second key, you'll first have to tell them who you are giving it to. Here, the lock maker takes responsibility and logs its keys. The keying system is so complex and out of the scope of this book that I prefer not to discuss it here. It wouldn't do the emergency lock picker any good, anyway.

Pick resistance: I rate this lock at **12.5**, not only because it is just better than the Ruko, but because it is so good that it has to fill the gap between an even better lock (shown in the next chapter) made by the same company. Also, as of this printing, I have not been able to pick this lock. As such—if I may be so bold—all pin tumbler locks would seem to fall below the **13.0** range in pick resistance. Also, any lock rated at the **11.0** level and above acts as virtually pick-proof for the first two hours of non-violent attack, established by the current, up-to-date premise of this book. (Pick-resistance ratings above **13.0** are reserved for some of the newer rotary tumbler locks, electronic card/key locking systems, and mechanical and digital safe locks—some of which will be covered in later chapters as they require a broader-based knowledge of their operation.)

1. Sensei John Angelos, Boulder, CO, 1987
2. Compliments of René Larsen of Denmark
3. ASSA.

8

Isolated Keyed Tumbler Locks

Many unique locks have come and gone. It would be nice if there were a lock museum that housed exact replicas (if not the originals) of all the locks ever made. However, it would still be very difficult to trace the order in which the ultimate pin tumbler lock evolved. And, unbelievably, it is doubtful that this group of locks is the last word in high security.

If you are reading this chapter, you are well into maximum security (not the cell, I hope—locks, you know) because this lock is tops. Personally, I would not even try this next type of lock without first feeling out the Medeco line of security locks. I even thought about using my teeth (Harry Houdini's approach) to give me an edge on this lock—but that is not recommended. Even so, to the professional burglar, this lock is an enigma because this category of locks is in a class of its own: "Submitted for your approval . . . at the signpost up ahead, your next stop—the Twilight Zone."

In my drive to classify stuff, I could have entitled this chapter "Spooled/Mushroom *Springless* Multiple Row Dual-

Coded Side-Bar . . ." Well, I just had to shorten it somehow. But this is the real short of it:

When a tumbler locking system removes itself from the keyway as far as it possibly can, it becomes extremely difficult to pick. Take, for example, an old, simple safe. Its handle is attached to a "fence" or "bolt" that rides on the two or three disc tumblers, each having a notch or "gate." You can hear and even feel these gates when you put pressure on the handle and turn the dial driving the tumblers as they rub across the bolt. This makes it easy to deduce the combination. When these gates are aligned by dialing out the proper combination, the handle/bolt can drop into the gates and allow it to turn, opening the safe door. In newer safes, the last tumbler (or number dialed) directly operates the bolt. But the handle is attached to a separate mechanism that releases the door. The handle can't turn unless the bolt is retracted out of the way by the act of dialing that last number. In this way, the bolt is isolated from the act of turning the handle. This prevents one from feeling the tumblers directly by manipulating the tumblers against the bolt.[1]

In the same way, a superior pin tumbler lock would isolate its pins from the cylinder making it nearly impossible to manipulate the system open without the proper code or key because you cannot feel the effects of the tumblers that you are picking! There is little, if any, connection between the shearing force in the act of turning the cylinder (like that of the safe's handle) and the motion of the pins (the safe's discs) required to allow that shearing action to take place. The more of a buffer zone between the two actions, the more secure the system is going to be. And there is no other key-controlled lock that demonstrates the power of the principle of isolation than the ASSA Desmo.

THE ASSA DESMO PHARMACY CABINET LOCK

In 1995, Abloy and ASSA merged, forming the most powerful force in pick-resistant lock manufacturing known. Out of this merger came a concept lock that is like no other. The result was the ASSA Desmo, which made its debut in 1998. A similar lock—the ASSA Twin V-10 door lock is based in part on this principle. (Refer back to last chapter on the Twin V-10.)

The Desmo is used on drug carts in hospitals because of its restricted key control. As of 2000, the Desmo is also available for payphones in AT&T- and GTE (now Verizon)-type machines. The manufacturer claims 1 million different key codes per lock.[2] One peek down this keyway and Harry Houdini would hit the streets looking for a real job.[3]

This lock is stainless steel throughout—tumblers and all. But don't let the wide keyway fool you into a false sense of confidence.

This revolutionary lock uses either six or eight pins depending on the size of the locking function—cabinet or door. The maker claims that the lock can be extensively master keyed. The beefy key is constructed of silver nickel for long life. It is resistant to bending and breaking due to its heavy construction. The "V" notch on the top edge of the key bit is a key machine reference and hold-down point and also allows the side-bar spring guide pins to retract into this gap, holding the key into the lock.

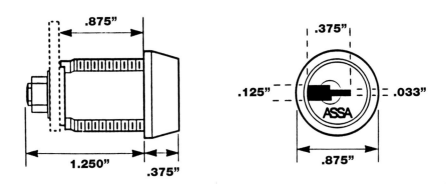

Figure 8A. The stainless steel ASSA Desmo is an isolated keyed tumbler lock that sets a higher standard in pharmaceutical cabinet and door locks.

The key slips into the lock so smoothly that operating this cylinder is virtually effortless. In fact, the key falls out of the tilted lock in the locked position. This is the most well-machined lock that I have ever encountered.

The ASSA Desmo incorporates a completely new locking technique based on directly driven pins. "The Precision Drive Pin System" operates independently of springs. According to an ASSA sales brochure, "The pins are 100-percent guided by the operation of the key." Being independent of the cylinder further isolates pins. Not being spring-loaded, the tumblers offer no feedback to your picking progress—it's like picking air. The Desmo dominates pharmaceutical locking applications because there is just no way that a person who is not firing on both hemispheres could open this lock by picking.

When I took this lock apart, I was at first disappointed. Is this all there is? I could not believe its simplicity. But when I saw all of the connections I realized why this lock is so good. Not only is the Desmo durable and reliable, it is amazingly simple. This is because the Desmo borrowed from past successful lock technologies:

- The Desmo pins—the main pick deterrent of the lock—are copied from the old reliable Yale lock (Chapter 2) spool pin technology of the last century;
- Like the TuBar discussed in Chapter 3, the Desmo demonstrates that two side-bars can fit into a cylinder;
- Also like the TuBar, it uses eight spooled pins with two false grooves;
- From the Medeco topless spooled pin side-bar locks described back in Chapter 5, the Desmo operates as a linear side-bar system with only one pin segment per chamber;
- This hybrid also uses the sides of the key to engage the tumblers rather than the edges, which is borrowed from the Ruko and ASSA V-10 designs detailed in Chapter 7.

The major difference between this lock and all of its ancestors is that it is springless, depriving lock pickers of getting the feedback they need.

Referring to Figure 8B, we see that the middle and bottom

sections of each pin are sleeved by the cylinder, making its travel very linear and smooth. But most amazingly, the pin damn near floats down when dropped into its pin chamber. There is no pin/cylinder shear line or any place where a tumbler can be felt when torque is applied to the cylinder.

The tumblers are offset from the keyway down its entire length. You can't even see a tumbler directly. Peering down the keyway, with the narrow end of the keyway up, is a miniature scene from Stephen King's *The Shining*. It's like looking down a stainless-steel hotel hallway with recessed doorways—four on each side. The pins, like the V-10, have "tabs" that protrude out of their sides at the bottom of the doorways, looking like sets of unknown shoes ready to leap out of the doors into the hall. (I've been told that I have a "rich inner life.")

Actually, these "tabs" are round, like one end of a weightlifter's dumbbell, with a single plate (as opposed to the top end of the pin, which looks like a stack of plates on the dumbbell). This bottom end of the pin is also heavily de-burred (no sharp edges) so as to accommodate the slots along the key. These key slots are "funneled" on the end of the key to pick up the tumbler "tabs" even if the lock is upside down.

The lower sides of the key have a machined groove that is one continuous slot that snakes along both sides of the key bit up to the bow. Each set of grooves is coded differently on each side of the key because this lock has two rows of these tumblers, one set on each side.

The lock's pins are entirely without springs (to wear out), yet when the lock is upside down the key slips smoothly into the keyway all the way back into the cylinder. Precision is the key to security and this lock has it.

At first glance at Figure 8B, one is reminded of a cutaway view of an eight-cylinder engine of some kind. But note the piston-like tumblers with what appear to be ring-grooves about their top ends. This is what spool pins have evolved into: a way to repeatedly (and most inconveniently) snag the pins while you are trying to pick them. Figure 8B shows these pins set into their side-bars with the lock unlocked. Basically, these grooves play direct interference with the link between the side-bar and the pins. This isn't new, though, as we discussed multi-spooled pins in the last chapter on the ASSA V-

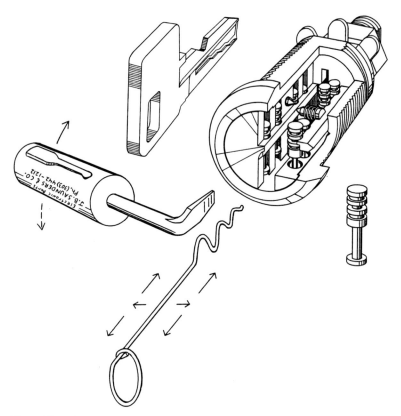

Figure 8B. Picking the ASSA Desmo with household items: A small, bent screwdriver tension wrench and wire snake rake. Rake in a "U" pattern: in left, out right; then in right, out left.

10. But here, all of the multi-spooled pins are not sheared. This almost totally isolates the pins from the action of the cylinder with the lock picks. If you haven't already guessed, the climax to this horror story is that there are two sets of side-bars.

At least with spring-loaded tumblers you get feedback of some sort. With this system, you really need to create the feedback system yourself somehow. In other words, short of using nanobots, this type of spool pin/side-bar arrangement actually requires at least three hands to pick it—one hand for the tension wrench and one hand each for the two spool pin/side-bar arrays. And, each of your three hands must know what the other two hands are doing while picking this lock and still act independently.

Each side-bar has only one spring, compressed only from the force of turning the key—another isolation feature. Note the beveled outer edge of the side-bar itself. When the right key is inserted into the cylinder and turned, this edge allows the side-bar to retract and slide into its recessed slot along the cylinder. Let's see if we can pick this lock. I've only tried it with the two-hand method (for various good reasons I wouldn't want to try it with a third) and unless you are an alien from the planet Oflybegon, you'll have to use the two-hand method too.

First, the lock must be mounted correctly, as depicted in Figure 8A. This is how our sample lock will be oriented for the picking procedure described. This is actually good, though, because gravity won't be working against you by letting the pins drop, plus, this is how they are mounted out in the field anyway. I have found the tools best for picking at this lock are the snake rake, pick "I" (as it can be used as a double tool, too—say that three times fast with popcorn in your mouth), and the looped Feather Touch ("M") tension wrench. (If you don't have this tool, you may try the small, bent screwdriver, with a .030" thick tip. You can grind it flat on your grinder. However, you'll need a lot of hand action with this type of wrench.) Set the tip of the wrench into the keyway at dead center of the cylinder face—in the thin slot section of the keyway. The handle of the wrench should be sticking out to the right of the keyway. Then gently slide the snake in along the top of the inner keyway, engaging the tumbler "tabs" hanging down.

As you draw the snake out, do so across the bottom set of pin "tabs." Be certain that you use very light tension pressure in the counter-clockwise direction and be sure that you are moving the pin tumbler tabs on both (up and down) rows of tumblers with a back and forth motion (in and out) with a gentle sideways action. As you are picking, go easy on the ten-sion-wrench force and only release the tension after making an unsuccessful pass at the tumblers with the snake. Take your time because you've got two sets of non-spring-loaded, ribbed pins controlling two side-bars to contend with.

Now, if you do not have a way to grind out the snake rake,[4] which is the recommended tool, you can make one by copying the pattern with stainless steel wire .040" diameter (18-gauge American Standard). You'll need a pair of small (5") round-nose pliers. Most hobby shops carry these for about $8. Don't grip the pliers tight or you'll mar, pinch, or even cut through the wire. Hold them loosely as you bend the wire into shape. It will take some practice, but after three or four tries, you'll have a dependable snake rake that will not break.

Pick resistance: For obvious reasons this lock is rated very high for a keyed tumbler system. As of this printing, I have not opened my two sample locks—each keyed differently. Because of the pick-resistance scale rating I have set up, this lock automatically falls into the rating of **13.0**—a rating that is still one full point beyond my present skill level, and may be considered "maximum pick resistance."[5]

So effectively, we have reached the top end of the food-chain in the evolution of the pin tumbler lock. Next, we explore what happens when a locking system flattens out its tumblers into discs and knocks the world of lockpicking on its butt by bringing back the combination disc safe lock—once again—but in miniaturized form.

1. See *Techniques of Safecracking*, Wayne B. Yeager, Loompanics Unlimited pp. 22-33. (Available through Paladin Press.)
2. According to ASSA, but, unless my math is messed up, I calculated fewer possibilities: 3 to the 8th power = 6,561. (Just like the eight-pin TuBar in Chapter 3.) But because of the nature of the lock, this doesn't really matter
3. No offense to H.H. fans—I have been a fan myself since 1965. But because of the impossibility of picking this lock in any position other than a mounted cylinder (gravity being the hindrance here) makes betting one's life on picking open this state-of-the-art lock a foolhardy endeavor.
4. The Snake rake design is taken from nature. In electronics, (and physics) an oscillating circuit will dampen (fade) out into smaller and smaller peaks when the power is removed. A dampened waveform is the natural tendency of any object in oscillation (being vibrated) or being cycled with repetitious linear movements (like raking a lock's tumblers) to follow a predictable pattern consistent with both mechanical and electrical systems. For more on the physics of oscillations, see the author's work *The Principles of Inertial Drive*, 1993, Appletree Press, <www.patentsecrets.com>.
5. Someday, someone will find a better way to pick open this lock. Perhaps it will be you! If you do, please write me and relay how you did it. I will make certain that you will be credited in our next book—but only if you really picked it. I will have to try your technique out myself before we can publish your name.

Keyed Disk Tumbler Locks

Some species devolve; the dolphin and whale were once land mammals that returned to the sea to better survive. They did this by re-adapting their systems to the long-lost environment to make their requirements for survival simpler and more direct. In a similar way, this next classification of locks has gone back to days past, when the disk tumbler safe lock ruled the world of security.

Remember Linus Yale Sr., the man mentioned at the beginning of this book who invented the pin tumbler lock? His son, Linus Yale Jr., was the man who invented the pin tumbler *cylinder* lock. Later, Junior went on to invent the rotary disk tumbler lock, the basic form of all safe locks for the past 150 years.

The Finnish company Abloy figured out how to use this basic principle of gated disk tumblers (while using only 1/4 of the disk's circumference[1]) and replaced the spindle and dial plate with a removable key. Thus was born the keyed disk tumbler lock, or "disklock." These locks are also springless.

105

The Keyed Disc Tumbler Principle:
Reinventing the Disc Safe Lock

1. *The key bit (shaft) acts like the spindle of a safe lock, while the key bow functions as the dial.*

2. *The tumbler carrier, an inner shell that carries the disc tumbler assembly when the proper key is inserted and turned, also guides the side-bar within the lock housing.*

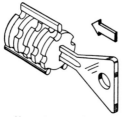

3. *With tumbler carrier removed and disc tumblers exposed, the key is inserted. It meets no resistance going into the keyway, as there are no spring-loaded parts.*

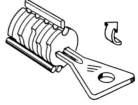

4. *When rotated 90 degrees (usually clockwise) with the proper key, the notches in the key bit pick-up each tumbler in turn and carry it until its gate aligns with the side-bar.*

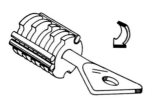

5. *With all of the disc tumblers aligned, the side-bar drops into place within the groove of the gates and disengages the plug assembly from the housing, opening the lock.*

6. *When turned back to its original position, the key may be removed. This action automatically scrambles the combination by the two return rollers.*

THE KEY DEVICES ROTARY TUMBLER LOCK

A popular keyed disklock in widespread use today is Key Devices' "rotary tumbler" lock, which is used in the gaming industry and for general-purpose locking applications. This American-made lock was invented by Francis E. Gallagher (U.S. Patent #4,838,055—1989), who also invented the lock in Figure 4B. It has nine disk tumblers that line up to a side-bar. The key is shaped as if it were a tube that was sliced down its length, making for a half-moon shaped keyway. (This is to prevent the use of flat tools to pick the lock.) Along its length are slots cut crosswise (perpendicular) that pick up the tumblers and align them to their proper places in various positions of up to 90 degrees.

In Figure 9B, the bottom tab on each tumbler (8A) is a stop that limits rotation to about 90 degrees within the tumbler carrier (7) and the notch on the outer circumference of the disk tumbler (8A) is its gate into which the side-bar drops (9). The half-moon slot in the center of the tumbler is where it rides the key. In this lock, about half of the disk tumblers are made of hardened steel while the other half are made of brass.

Like the last category of locks, the lack of tumbler springs makes this lock very tough to pick open. Since disklocks are keyed *through* the tumblers, instead of beneath or against them, and have no tumbler springs, a different approach is needed. Also, this is a side-bar lock, increasing the skill level needed to open it. But it can be opened by picking with some patience.

Because of the crescent-moon slots and the close proximity of the disk tumblers to one another, a standard diamond pick is too wide on its end to effectively engage these disk tumblers. The best tool for tagging the disks is the L-pick (see tool "J," Figure 1C). In order to see which tumbler you are picking, etch spacing marks of .050" apart on the pick's shaft so that you can easily gauge where you are. You may use an inexpensive electric engraving tool from your local hardware

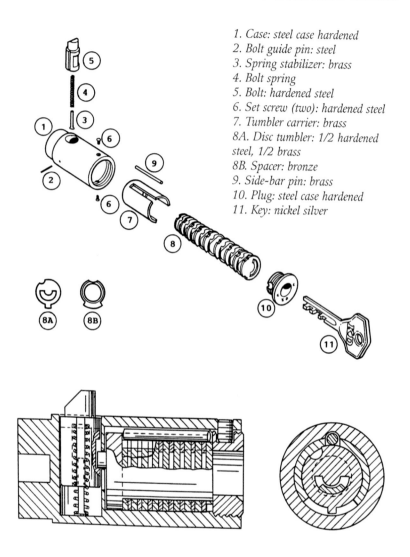

1. Case: steel case hardened
2. Bolt guide pin: steel
3. Spring stabilizer: brass
4. Bolt spring
5. Bolt: hardened steel
6. Set screw (two): hardened steel
7. Tumbler carrier: brass
8A. Disc tumbler: 1/2 hardened steel, 1/2 brass
8B. Spacer: bronze
9. Side-bar pin: brass
10. Plug: steel case hardened
11. Key: nickel silver

Figure 9B. Key Devices' nine-disc tumbler lock: Brass and hard steel tumblers are sandwiched to deter drilling. Note that there are seven different metals involved in the making of this lock and key.

store, or you can carefully scribe the marks with a carbide-tip scribe for a several dollars less. The latter will also allow you to have more control over your scribe marks. Don't etch too deep or you'll weaken the metal shaft of the L-pick. Use about the same force as printing your name. Even just a light scratch will last a lifetime.

On some disk tumbler locks, the last mark closest to the handle should stop at the opening of the keyway when the pick is all the way into the lock. The first mark should measure .100" from the end of the tool so that you do not etch right at the short end of the L, as this will weaken the tool at its most vulnerable place. There should be 15 of these .050"-spaced marks on your metered L-pick.

Figure 9C. With a carbide-tip tool engraver, meter your lock pick "J" for picking rotary tumbler locks. Etch lines .050" apart.

Also, a regular tension wrench will not work in the C-shaped keyway; the hole is too wide and that's not the way this lock works. When the key (11) operates the lock, the bit's end actually engages the last tumbler at the back of the keyway where it is the first to turn and the last to engage the tumbler carrier (7) with its stop tab. Its gate is also the last to align with the side-bar (9).

Because there are no tumbler springs and no need of an external tension wrench, we can set each tumbler one at a time and they will stay where we moved them with the pick. Lock pick "J" is also a unique tool, as it must rotate the tumbler instead of pushing it. This is why the pick must be metered—so that we can tell which tumbler it is rotating. This tool was also designed to be long enough to accommodate the 13-tumbler lock.

The internal tension wrench is the unmetered pick "J,"

and you want to run it back deep into the lock until you bottom out. Then you want to pull out the pick one tumbler's width—about 1/16 of an inch. Use a relatively firm, twisting motion to engage the last tumbler in the lock. This tumbler actually drives the tumbler carrier (7). Here, you will be turning clockwise and forcing the sidebar to contact the tumblers.

There are two methods I used to pick this lock. The first method is called the One-Pick Method. It involves one L-pick used as both a pick and wrench. Start by inserting it at the entrance of the keyway and turn each tumbler clockwise a few degrees until you hit the very back of the lock, where you engage the tumbler carrier. When you bottom out here, pull out 1/16″ and turn with the very same L-pick, using slightly more pressure, and you'll feel the tumbler carrier mechanism give a little. If it stops, then you need to re-position some disks. Carefully remove the pick without moving any disks and re-insert it again to repeat the process. You can even turn counterclockwise occasionally in case you moved a disk too far. Each pass, go to the back of the lock and try again to turn the tumbler carrier at the rear. This is a random method and is dependent upon one's good karma.

A better approach is the Two-Pick Method. You need two L-picks for this method, which is faster but requires more skill. Again, pick "J" is the best tool for the job, but you don't need to meter this one, as you will be using it like a tension wrench. But instead of using it as a rotator hook wrench as we would on the Van lock in Chapter 3, we want to use this tool as an L-pick like on warded and lever locks.

Unlike most side-bar locks, there will be a little resistance to the disk tumbler as it approaches the side-bar, because the other disks are not being forced to work against the side-bar with their springs—the disks have no springs. So in a sense, being springless here is to the lock-picker's slight advantage.

This is an advantage because the ends of these keys are never cut. This means that the last tumbler is the first to move when the key is turned and the last tumbler to align with the side-bar and engage the carrier with its tab. (Refer back to

Figure 9A, sections four and five.) By picking the lock in this fashion, you will be forcing the tumbler carrier to bind against the side-bar and tumblers so that they can be more easily felt when their gates align. There is a slight relief in the wrench and pick as well. Note that five different metals are used in the making of this lock, and different metal densities will dampen picking sounds much to the lock's advantage. For example, the steel tumblers will sound and feel differently when aligning than will the brass tumblers. So you will have to listen and feel very attentively. A magnetically-mounted stethoscope would be a great help in picking this lock: Mount a ring-shaped disc magnet to a medical stethoscope using a good silicone-based adhesive.

Run the L-wrench all the way into the lock until it stops, pull out 1/16″ and turn slightly. You'll feel the tumbler carrier give a little. When picking this method you search the tumblers with the metered L-pick like in the One-Pick Method, but instead of having to bottom out the metered L-pick, you have the other, unmetered L-pick already inserted at the back of the lock applying tension on the tumbler carrier. Once all of the tumblers are aligned in this fashion, the picks must be removed and a small screwdriver is then needed to carefully turn the very first tumbler in the front of the lock to operate the cam at the rear.

Pick resistance: I spent hours picking at this disk tumbler lock. When it finally popped, I lost track of the time. But, by using the Two-Pick Method, I popped it in about 30 minutes. This lock is rated above pin tumbler locks in general because of the skill needed to manipulate the individual disk tumblers into a static position unseen and essentially unfelt within the cylinder. However, this lock is relatively easy to mass produce in that the disks can be stamped out with only about four different patterns, making it inexpensive to the consumer. So, though this lock is relatively simple in design and function, the Key Device's rotary disk lock is still rated high on the pick scale: **10.0.**

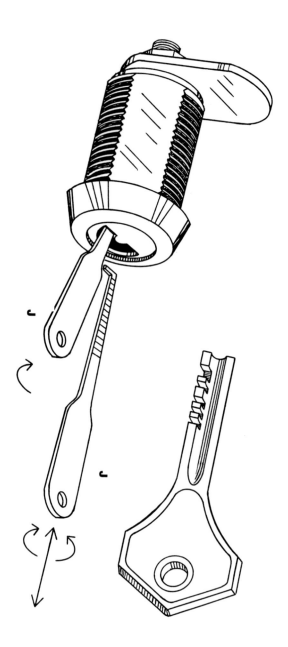

Figure 9D. Picking a keyed disc tumbler lock with two L-picks: one as tension wrench, the other metered to gauge and rotate the disc tumblers.

THE ABLOY CLASSIC (PULLDOG)

This beauty has been around for some time. The Abloy disklock principle was invented 1906, however, the Finnish lock did not hit American markets until 1980s where I had seen it used on coin operated washers and dryers. This lock was called to my attention by another reader[2] several years ago. It has tighter machine tolerances than the Key Devices rotary.

Because of its uniqueness, it is now also being used on soda machines, padlocks, and as door locks. The Abloy Classic "Pulldog" Disklock uses seven to nine disk tumblers that rotate 90 degrees in a clockwise direction to allow a side-bar (familiar theme?) to drop, clearing the housing so that the cylinder (in this case the tumbler carrier) can rotate. The maker claims 1.97 billion possible combinations.

The later models (Abloy Exec and Pro series) have disks with a "false gate" that is a shallow cut along its edge to confuse picking attempts. But each disk must be turned only a certain distance before aligning with the side bar. And since they are not spring-loaded, it is possible to rotate each disk individually, but you cannot rotate the whole plug without a contiguous link between all nine disks; this is accomplished by the tumbler carrier. The side-bar must drop into each disk's "true gate" indentation. You can identify the Abloy Pulldog locks by the half-moon shaped key hole. On the newer Abloy Profile, in the center of the keyhole is a tab that gives the keyway the appearance of a comma (,). The difference between the two locks is a more restricted and smaller keyway on the Profile. Both cylinders turn clockwise; in fact, nearly all keyed disk tumbler locks unlock clockwise, unless they are special ordered. (Also, an important note: *All* cylinder padlocks—no matter what type or brand—unlock clockwise.) It is Abloy who is dominating the padlock and small box locking niches of the market. But they have recently broken into the door-lock market quite successfully with their later disklock models, Abloy Exec and the Abloy Disklock Pro, which we may cover in another book.

A typical tension wrench and metered L-pick method described above for Key Devices rotary tumbler locks is especially tedious and very time-consuming with this lock. The reason? The fine machining, the false gates, and the fact that all tumblers must be engaged at once before any torque can be applied to rotate the plug to unlock this lock. This is because there is a very snug side-bar that must be engaged by all of the tumblers, making false gates more effective. Also, the spacers rotate, too, making one uncertain whether he's turning a disk or a spacer. There just had to be a better way to open this type of lock.

One day, while reminiscing, I remembered my early days as a locksmith apprentice out in the field making keys for customers who were locked out of their cars or had lost their car keys. We would use blank keys for that particular auto lock—most of which were GM side-bar wafer locks—and file a functioning key on the spot. This practice is called "impressioning a key." So, why not "impression" a key for the disk tumbler lock as well? But where would you get the key blanks? I immersed myself into this question while gazing at a roll of copper tubing.

Duh.

One of my Abloy Classics then slipped open after I had impressioned a key made from a piece of the copper tube.

First, acquire a copper tube measuring .250" (1/4") in diameter (a standard size.) Cut off a four- to five-inch length and bend it halfway down at 90 degrees, as illustrated. If you have medium to large hands, bend only to 45 degrees, as this will reduce impressioning torque with a lesser chance of breaking off the tool in the lock.

Carefully grind it flat on one side—halfway down into and along the length, as shown. Quench frequently in water to anneal the copper to keep it from becoming too soft. Then lightly sand the bright red copper along the two flat edges with a fine, 220-grit sanding paper on a flat surface until the edges are smooth and shiny. Finish up the edge by folding a sheet of paper over the edge of a hard-surfaced table and stroking the flat across the paper to polish it up.

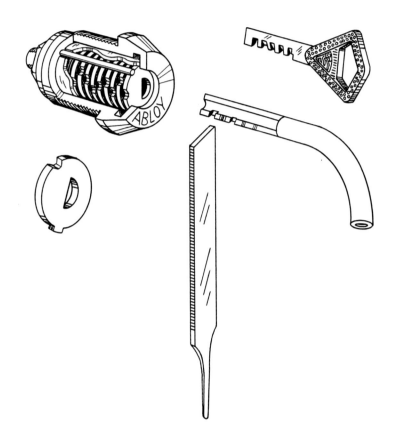

Figure 9E. Impressioning a rogue key for a keyed disc tumbler lock: An edge file cuts the marks left behind by the disks on the bisected copper tubing.

Insert the C-shaped, cross-sectioned copper tube into the keyway to the back of the lock (the Abloy Classic does not have a 1/16″ gap at the rear of the tumbler stack like the Key Devices rotary). Now gently turn it clockwise until it binds. Release the pressure and remove the "blank key." You should see some tumbler scratch marks, or even polished shiny marks, on the leading edge along the length of the blank. There should be a mark near the end of your blank, which will be the last tumbler, along with a few other marks. The force of turning the makeshift key makes the round side-bar of the lock bind against the tumblers and copper tubing edge. Since copper is softer than steel, bronze, and brass, tumblers will dig into it and leave a mark. These marks will be very light and shiny, and thin lines will be visible running perpendicular across the edge of the cut copper tube. Other marks from the rest of the tumblers will show up further into the process, but sometimes, all nine (or 11) marks may be visible at first and they will all be evenly spaced. The spacing will remain the same throughout the process—about .035" wide for tumblers and .020" for spacers. But the depth of the marks will depend on the code of the lock.

With a small, 6" long by 1/4" wide flat-edged file (with a 3/64" or slightly smaller working face), remove the marks until they are no longer visible—do not file more than what is required to remove the mark. File lightly straight across and in one direction on each tumbler position mark. Copper is very soft, so don't get carried away with the file; use your thumb and forefinger to hold the file and use light strokes in one direction to avoid see-sawing the file and rounding your cuts. A few light strokes per mark are enough. Though it is not shown in figure 9E, it may help to keep your filing even by filing both edges—using the other edge of the tube to support your file. This will not affect opening the lock in the clockwise direction but will not be useful should the lock unlock in the counterclockwise direction.

Once you have filed away the light tumbler marks, re-insert the cut-away tube and carefully turn again to bind the tumblers, repeating the process over again. *Do not file where there are no marks in the spots where you have already filed.* If all tumbler marks are the same depth after several cycles of filing, you may be going the wrong direction—get a fresh blank and go counterclockwise. There are a few odd-ball locks out there and some customers, if they are smart, order reversed cylinder locks for added security. Eventually, the half-tube key will align all of the tumblers and the cylinder will turn, tightly at first. But stop, pull out, and re-file any new marks before turning any further. You are only a few tries away from making a fully functional key. This is how you can impression a keyed disk tumbler key. Note that this is not a durable key—temporary at best—and you will have to be careful not to twist the copper tube key off into the lock. To help prevent this while turning the unlocked cylinder, relieve pressure on the cam by pushing in on the locked door.

Copper is ductile (soft, flexible) enough to withstand much bending. However, again, when making this tool, be sure to quench the tube in water while cutting it lengthwise every 1/4-inch or so. Also dunk in water every 10 seconds of grinding the flat cross-section. This will keep the copper from gumming up your grinding wheel.

Pick resistance: The Two-Pick Method mentioned above for the Key Devices rotary tumbler lock should open this one, but I couldn't do it with my sample. But here, the impressioning process to open this lock does not reduce its security factor because the above technique requires enough skill to make it secure against common thieves. It also takes a good deal of time and bright, full spectrum light to see the marks, making exposure too risky. I would rate the Abloy Classic at a good **10.5**.

THE ABLOY PROFILE DISKLOCK

This lock can also be opened by impressioning. Repeat the technique detailed above for the Classic, but use 1/4" aluminum tubing. The tubing walls are thinner, making the I.D. (inner diameter) larger so that it can easily slip past the displaced center tab of the Profile's comma-shaped keyway to impression a "tube-key." Aluminum is also softer than copper and makes only a fair key, but is much more "gummy" when it comes to machining the substance. Use less force and more water when cutting and grinding your flats on this material. Spray water on the grindstone while cutting to prevent material drag along fresh-cut surfaces. Carefully and very lightly

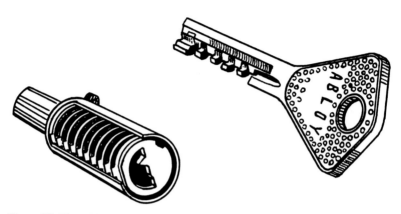

Figure 9F. The Abloy Profile disklock IC fits into padlock housings. The key engages the tumblers clockwise into the tight, restricted area of the keyway, making the impressioning of a rogue key more difficult.

file away the soft splinters along the face that will engage the tumblers to leave marks. Caution: to avoid getting aluminum splinters in your eyes, rinse your hands in running water after completing this procedure.

Pick resistance: Since the material used to impression a rogue key is softer, the skill-level also increases a bit. So the Abloy Profile is rated a little higher: **11.0**.

This is the last chapter covering the purely mechanical tumbler locks. We have followed the evolution of the pin tumbler lock from its divergence from wafer locks (to be covered in my next book) and its cousin, the disk tumbler lock with its slower, but significant, climb up the ladder of higher security. After the safe was developed in the middle 1800s, the next development in the line of defense against the night thief was electronic alarm systems. So logically, in the remaining chapters we will explore the latest in electronic locking systems.

1. *Secrets of Lock Picking,* pp. 49-54.
2. Compliments of Frank Pittman, St. Augustine, Florida.

10

Electronic Key Locks

When it comes to security, just the word "electronic" scares most people. And it is surprising just how little most people know about true "electronics"—the functioning guts of video, audio, and computer circuits. The average person has enough to contend with just living everyday life, which is also filled with things that are electronic in function (which helped to cause all of the stress with coping in the first place).

Well, if it is of any help, no one can define on the molecular level why a transistor works (in any certain terms), but it works. Invented by three men at Bell Labs in 1947, this simple, silicon-based switch—the transistor—makes everything run in this world (this position was formerly held by the vacuum tube). In fact, we have become so dependent on this little switch, that the world could not function without it.[1]

Few people could tell you how this "solid-state" switch can be used to convert AC (alternating current) from the wall socket in our house into DC (direct current) for autos and making our televisions and stereos function—which is the basic operation of a simple DC power supply. In fact, the average person doesn't even know the difference between AC and DC, for that matter, or how simple solid-state switches evolved into mega-microprocessing circuits occupying a cubic quarter-inch area. But this is also the intended direction of high security: *Security is dependent upon the ignorance of the masses.* However, security must evolve to keep up with the "Information Age."

In order for us to fully grasp the significance of the technology now ruling modern security, let us consider the next series of new locking systems.

SECURITRON DUAL ALARM SWITCH/DOOR LOCK

The now all-powerful ASSA/Abloy Group has acquired another company called Securitron Magnalock, which features high-quality electronic security hardware and systems. One product they manufacture that caught my eye is the dual alarm/door switch. The stainless steel plate looks like any other electrical box cover plate except that there is a mortise cylinder mounted on it and the plate is held with tamper-proof screws. Now, this looks like a normal electric door lock; you insert your key and turn the cylinder, activating a switch to release the solenoid bolt with a "clack" and unlock the door. Note that these electric "strikes" (electrically controlled dead bolts) cannot be pried open with a knife as with a spring-loaded latch. A large crowbar might be a match for a few of them. But most are made with hardened steel and interlock vertically with their mating half, making crowbarring an act of utter futility.

In any case, the Securitron Dual Alarm Switch device gives you a 50/50 chance to get it right the first time or an alarm will trip.

The cylinder can be anything: a standard pin tumbler, radial pin tumbler, a Medeco, or even an Abloy disklock. Furthermore, clockwise may unlock the electric solenoid-controlled bolt to open the door and counterclockwise may

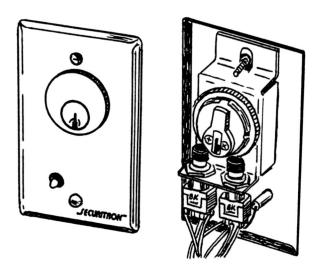

Figure 10A. The Securitron Dual Keyswitch. An electric deadbolt and alarm switch makes picking the lock twice as risky.

turn off the alarm, or, is it the other way around? A burglar could inadvertently unlock the door and walk right into the police station.

The point is, you have to pick the cylinder twice—once to snap the switch "off" on the left for the alarm (but, could be wired for the door) then pick it right to unlock the electric door lock (but, could be the alarm's "on" switch). If, perchance, the alarm was already turned off, you could pick the lock to inadvertently snap it back on, setting your own trap. It's a Catch-22: damned if you do, and damned if you do.

Furthermore, this simple system can be changed on the spot by the owner. He simply reverses the position of the switches should he lose a questionable employee (and change the lock too, if he's wise).

One approach might be to pick it in one direction to activate the bolt, in which case you would hear the clack of the electric door strike. Then, pick the cylinder again in the opposite direction to disable the alarm, then pick it back again in the previous direction to unbolt the door again. The strike (or bolt) switch is only a momentary switch, which means once you release the cylinder, it re-locks. But this process means that you might have to pick that cylinder three times. If the cylinder is an Abloy disklock, you could be there all night. If the lock is an ASSA Twin V-10, you could be there for three to five years.

The foggy white or translucent button on the lower left of the face plate is actually a bi-color LED lamp; the green light is for enter and open and the red light means locked and alarm on. (Or is that the other way around? Just joking.)

In any case, I thought that this simple system is a good one and worth mentioning, but there is no pick resistant rating for it because the lock could be anything.

THE RUKO TWINTRONIC
MAX SECURITY BANK DOOR LOCK

The Ruko, a multi-row spooled pin tumbler side-bar lock, has a sophisticated version of its already complex security features—the Ruko Twintronic,[2] which also incorporates an additional side-bar (making it also a multi side-bar lock), which is controlled by an electronic recognition system within the cylinder and key.

You are already familiar with the lock mechanism from our trials in Chapter 7. But in this version, there is the added security feature involving electronics. The key bow contains (in counter-clockwise fashion from upper left) a tiny push-button switch that turns on a micro-oscillator circuit (below) with its tuned inductor (above and right of switch). In the top edge of the key bow is a tiny ferrite rod antenna that broadcasts a frequency to match the pick-up coil at the top front and just beneath the surface of the cylinder face (the ring-shaped loop above the cylinder). The pick-up coil relays its signal out to a remote receiver box through the electronics and connector (the plug running out the back of the lock housing), which can send back an electrical current to release

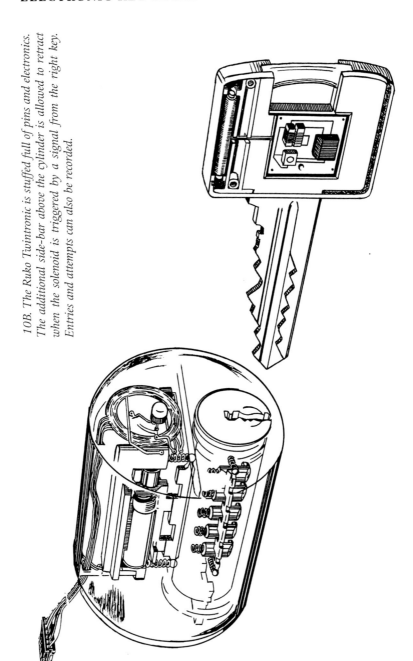

10B. The Ruko Twintronic is stuffed full of pins and electronics. The additional side-bar above the cylinder is allowed to retract when the solenoid is triggered by a signal from the right key. Entries and attempts can also be recorded.

the tiny solenoid controlled side-bar (just above the main pin springs in the cylinder). When the solenoid-coil energizes and slides forward, the side-bar is free to rise under the force of the turning cylinder after all 11 pins have been properly aligned. The system can also log in when and who (individual key holder identity) gained entrance.

In the Ruko, the key contains its own power source—a long-life (10+ years) miniature battery. The small protrusion above the keyway and centered in the pick-up coil is a bi-color LED lamp indicating status of the cylinder. Red is locked and green indicates that the key is accepted and the cylinder is free to turn. These locks have been used primarily on European industrial applications and bank doors since the 1980s. Though still in wide use in Europe, the Ruko company went out of business in the middle 1990s. However, ASSA is now making replacement ICs for the existing Ruko cylinders whenever re-keying is required.

This basic type of electronic system (excluding the data logging circuits) is also being used in some of the new automobile locks manufactured today.

The usual electronic jamming method employed on magnetic card readers[3] will not work on these systems, as each unit is programmed to receive only its computer-coded frequency from the proper key. All other frequencies and pulses are filtered out by the mainframe electronics of the system. Then you have all those tumblers to deal with . . .

Pick resistance: Naturally, this lock is near pick-proof with all that stuff crammed into it. This type of system is **14.0**.

This ends our excursion on keyed tumbler locks. Note that we have reached near the top end of my arbitrary pick-resistance scale. The next logical classification of locks will be the ones that can be truly called "lockpick-proof" because they use numerical combinations rather than physical keys. Here, dexterity gives way to wits.

---

1. For more about electronic security systems, see the author's *Affordable Security*, Paladin Press.
2. Compliments of René Larsen of Denmark.
3. *Advanced Lock Picking Secrets*, Paladin Press.

Electronic Combination Locks

People die. Combinations are lost. As a locksmith, you may be called out to open a digital push-button door or safe lock. You could call the manufacturer, but he can't give you the code because the serial number of the lock is not available to you because the owner neglected to fill out and mail his registration card. Or the serial number either melted off in the fire, is locked inside the safe, or just plain wore off with age. But you actually have two options. You could blow the lock and possibly damage it beyond ever opening again and risk damaging the contents, or you can pop it with logic.

I've had to open several safes because of deaths; the added distractions of grief and expectation can be annoying. The worst case involved the reading of a will (locks open much easier when you are not under pressure). So to master this skill requires more than just a basic knowledge of locks and electronics.

Most sane people would never attempt to bypass a digital electronic security system. And fortunately for everyone,

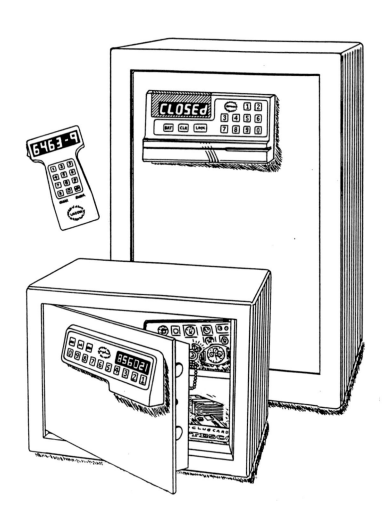

Figure 11A. Ilco Unican's Solitaire Series 200 hotel room safe is about as safe as you can get away from home. Most digital combinations can be deduced by using the most familiar numbers, logic, or footprints.

maybe only one in a million people would have the aptitude, patience, or skill to decipher and outwit digital combination locks. Most of the main-line hotels now have rooms with safes shielded by digital combination locks. In fact, you can go down to your local Staples office supply store and buy a safe with a digital combination lock with a key controlled backup[1] for around $250.

ILCO UNICAN SOLITAIRE 200 HOTEL ROOM SAFE

The Ilco Unican Solitaire 200 series features convenience and security in its new line of small hotel room safes. The Solitaire 200 is a solid, battery-powered, maintenance-free, user-friendly "intelligent" safe. (It even has a lighted interior.)

The computerized locking system allows guests to lock the safe with either a credit card or personal identification number (PIN). Each time the safe is locked, the same card or PIN must be used to open it. The safe will not lock on low battery. In the event of lost cards or forgotten codes, a master card or master PIN can be programmed into each safe and used to override a locked unit.[2]

A handheld override module is used to open all safes, regardless of the way they were locked. This separate unit has its own power source and is independent of the master card or the PIN in use.[3] As far as losing memory with loss of battery power, integrated circuit chips now have long-time residual memories. But usually, you have to re-program the combination after the battery has been replaced or you cannot lock the safe door—a consumer consideration most appreciated.

Hotel managers have access to a 12-event audit and can program up to eight operating functions to meet their hotel's specific needs. Factory programmed site codes prevent the use of unauthorized (rogue) override modules.[4] This means that a successful rogue module must also be programmed to match the additional secret code that only the factory has a record of.

Most of the newer systems can pick up commands via infrared laser to rewrite the safe's combination. The codes that are transmitted vary from manufacturer to manufacturer.

Note that this is not a fire-resistant safe (which usually has concrete between the walls). But that's OK because most hotels have a sprinkler system of some sort. In Figure 11A, the upright safe model 202 is "briefcase size" (22"x 15"x 14") and weighs 103 pounds. The safe model 201 in the foreground is "laptop" size and measures 11"x 16"x 13," weighing in at around 33 pounds.

The override module (200-1) will work only on the safes that it is programmed to work on, so there is no known "magic circuit" that will open all of these models of safes. Ripping off the electronic keypad would ensure that the door remains locked. But, since they are just small safes with 5/16"- and 1/4"-thick doors, more primitive safecracking methods can be employed. In this volume, we are interested only in the locking mechanism—not in classic safecracking techniques—because this type of lock on a larger safe would make it quite formidable.

There are two methods used to crack codes for digital locks on doors and computer programs. For the first, you'll need to know something about the person who chose the safe's combination. People by nature are forgetful—in this modern world there is just too much to remember. The most common practice used by the citizens to ensure not finding themselves locked out is to use familiar numbers. Numbers relating to the birthdays of children, one's spouse, or self are often used as combination codes. So are Social Security numbers, addresses, phone numbers (real stupid), and, yes, even driver's license numbers. Even I was once dumb enough to use my old military service number on a manuscript safe. But the real winners use their winning lottery ticket number. And the really clever chap might use any of the above series of personal numbers in reverse fashion.

By the way, if you have to come up with a combination, you are best off if you force yourself to sit down and memorize a new series of random digits by writing it over and over on a single sheet of paper (not on a note pad). Then, put it in a safe place for a week to be certain that you have memorized it. Then burn the paper.

The second technique to defeat digital locks is dirty. Most digital encoding pads used to punch-in codes allowing entry are heavily used, and the dirt from dozens of people's fingers can accumulate quickly on the pad numbers, leaving behind "footprints." Most people would not think to keep these pads clean, but the numbers that have the most dirt around them are the code numbers that the professional burglar would track. Wear patterns are another problem, and once he has those three or four digits, he can try out a series of combinations that would allow him to open the lock within one to three minutes.

For example, suppose you have a customer with a lost combination to an entrance keypad that had three digits that seemed to have a halo of light scum around the numbers 3, 5, and 7. To reduce the risk of losing the footprints, punch your try-out codes with a retracted ink pen or toothpick, just in case you read your numbers wrong. Let's see how you would work the try-out combinations. First, treat the combination like a whole number (357) with the smallest number first. Then try that combination. Next, swap the last two digits in the base number to 375 and try it. Next, shift the hundreds from 3 to the next number up, which is 5, and use the same procedure with those numbers: 537 and 573. Then shift the hundreds again to 7, which is 735 and 753. So, let's review:

357, 375
537, 573
735, 753

Out of a possible 999 combinations to open that lock, it is quickly narrowed down to six possible combinations. Scary, ain't it? Of course, a four-digit combination ups the ante by four-fold to 24 possible combinations out of 9,999. But still . . .

And, logically, if one button is half as "clean" as the rest (or twice as dirty, depending upon one's outlook on life), then that digit is used twice. For example, if 3 looked dirtier than only one other key, say 5, then we would get: 335, 353, 533. Just three possible combinations! Ten seconds and we're in.

Now, let's look at what most keypads use—four digits. Let's say that you have found four digits dirty or worn: 3, 5, 7, and 9. Now, we have to work in thousands, as well as hundreds. First, break the base number 3579 into four groups of a thousand with the first group using 3 in the thousand's place and swap the last two digits:

3579, 3597

Then, within that thousands group, shift the hundreds, smallest numbers first, and swap the last two digits again:

3759, 3795

Then, work your way up through the numbers like so:

3957, 3975

See? Then shift up to the next thousands group of 5 from your base number like so:

5379, 5397, 5739, 5793, 5937, 5973

Next thousands group of 7:

7359, 7395, 7539, 7593, 7935, 7953

And lastly, the 9 thousands group:

9357, 9375, 9537, 9573, 9735, 9753

These are the total possible codes from four digits: Just

24! This is because we are only using the digits, not all of the possible numbers in between those digits. *You can use this technique with any four-digit combination* as long as those numbers are not being used 2 or more times.

Best defense: keep the keypad clean and replace it when worn keys appear. Some companies now feature a keypad with "hardened" buttons to help solve the wear problem. But regular cleaning will ensure better security. Also, one should not use the same number more than once in a three- or four-digit code, as this lowers your security by a factor of at least four.

Digital safe combination locks can be deduced in this way as well: Here, with three to four sets of double digits, the possible combinations can range up into thousands—a few hours work, once a thief has crunched the numbers by computer. Well worth most burglars' efforts.

Pick resistance: If the keypads are kept clean and have wear-resistant keys, and the combination is random, this type of lock is virtually pickproof. I know of no other way to open a digital combination lock outside of knowing the combination from "footprints" or having access to the hand-held encoder system. But, digital combination locks still have one more major security design flaw that is inherent and unavoidable. It is only because of the next electronic lock mentioned in this book, (which solves the above problems) that I can place digital push-button locks in general on the PR scale of between **13.5** to **14.5**.

THE HIRSCH SCRAMBLE PAD SYSTEM

Burglars and street thugs will often peer—sometimes with binoculars—over the shoulder of their intended victims while they are having quality time with their ATMs. Now, with high-powered video cameras, they can decipher bank account numbers, PINs, and even (Lord forbid) Social Security numbers.

Your Social Security number is one code that should be sacred to you. Do not give it out freely. Do not have it printed on your driver's license. Do not have it printed on your checks: With it, a crook (anyone) can have access to your whole life—bank account numbers, credit card accounts, driver's license number, military service records, police records (if any), even your Social Security benefits, should you be alone and happen to die. If your Social Security number gets out you would be exposed. Social Security number theft doesn't happen often, but it does happen. Also, I have a few acquaintances who have had their Social Security numbers "borrowed" by persons on the run or covering their trails, causing them a variety of problems.

Crooks can get all of this information just by watching you, usually from a distance, as you punch in your personal numbers. Since most keypads don't change, it is relatively easy to decode keypad positions and sequence the numbers punched in from the videotape, or live with binoculars. This sort of crime happens quite frequently.

The Hirsch Scramble Pad solves the problems described above, both code number deduction through skin debris and/or keypad button wear and keypad pattern recognition (peeping).

The digits are LED displays within each keypad number position. Every time a code is punched in, and the system allows entry or access to cash, etc., it scrambles—at random—the next display on the buttons. This makes it impossible for a thief to peer over your shoulder and see your code through pattern recognition. By the time he gets to the keypad, the digits have already changed position. Also, all of the keypad buttons wear evenly, making it impossible to deduce a code.

The maker advertises that the system eliminates the cost and maintenance of cards or other physical credentials. This is the wave of the future. The system is microprocessor based with more than 111 million random code possibilities. The latest version of the system interfaces with conventional card readers and upgrades the readers to dual technology.

Here, no wear pattern develops on the buttons. Vertical and horizontal light guides narrow the viewing field so only one person standing directly in front of the keypad can see the display.

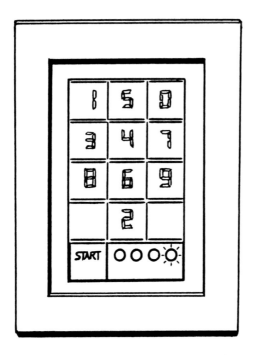

Figure 11B. The Hirsch Scramble Pad is the last word in modern security. The digits change position after each use and built-in viewing guards prevent peeping.

The Hirsch Scramble Pad uses a PIN code of three to four digits. The system administrator can assign the digits or let the system controller randomly generate them. The manufacturer also points out:

"Use of memorized credentials means that an individual cannot leave the credential at home, as often happens with cards. Nor can another person copy the credential without the owner's knowledge. Since the credential is so secure and traceable to its owner, it is not likely to be loaned out, a constant risk with card technologies. Thus each user is held accountable for his/her individual code use."

The keypad face is one-piece molded to prevent tampering, but just in case, the pad has a tamper alarm system.

Someday soon, this system will be more commonplace. I

have no intention in even trying to figure out how to crack this system—and even if I did know how, I wouldn't tell for obvious reasons.

Pick resistance: Currently, there is no known technique for bypassing this type of system short of using ESP while someone is punching in a code. Today, it represents the ultimate in pick resistance for keyless entry door locks and is rated at **15.0**.

1.   A key-controlled backup for a digital safe fully defeats the purpose of having the digi-lock in the first place. I find this silly and a waste of money.
2.   Ilco Unican Electronics Division.
3.   Ibid.
4.   Ibid.

Conclusion

We have seen how the simple pin tumbler lock has changed and developed into the complex systems that are on the market today. But it is more than obvious that this race for security is not over. As I write these last few pages, I am looking down at a growing pile of sample high-security locks yet to be opened. So please keep watching Paladin for upcoming books exploring more intriguing new locks.

SEND ME YOUR LOCK DISCOVERIES!

I would like to thank you, the reader, for the inspiration to write this book. This manual would not have come about had it not been for you.

Therefore, I would like to empower you to write and send me photographs or photocopies of any new lock that I have not yet covered in this or previous works. Foreign locks are especially welcome. A good photocopy of a sales brochure will suffice (please send a copy of the whole brochure, with the manufacturer's phone and address, please). Also, we are interested in old, odd-ball, and otherwise rare locks for another book. In all cases, a U.S. patent number would be very helpful. Sometimes they are stamped along the backside or front rim of the lock. Who knows? Your name and city might get printed as a footnote in our next locksmith's manual. Please send lock discoveries to:

Steven Hampton
c/o Paladin Press
Gunbarrel Tech Center
7077 Winchester Drive
Boulder, CO 80301
No phone calls or faxes, please.

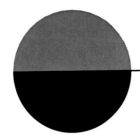

Bibliography

Hampton, Steven. *Advanced Lock Picking Secrets*. Boulder, CO: Paladin Press, 1989.

_____. *Secrets of Lock Picking*. Boulder, CO: Paladin Press, 1987.

_____. *Patent Secrets: How You Can Protect Your Invention for as Little as $25*. Boulder, CO: Paladin Press, 2000.

_____. *The Principles of Electromagnetic Inertial Drive*. Boulder, CO: Appletree Press, 1993.

Minnery, John. *Pick Guns: Lock Picking for Spies, Cops, and Locksmiths*. Boulder, CO: Paladin Press, 1989.

Yeager, Wayne B. *Techniques of Safecracking*. Port Townsend, WA: Loompanics Unlimited, 1990.

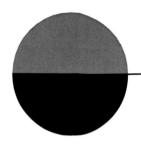

About the Author

In the summer of 1963, 12-year-old Steven Hampton became foster child to a Midwestern dairy farming couple. He fed, cleaned, and helped milk 50 cows twice daily while also going to school. At the age of 14, Steven acquired a set of U.S. Air Force electronic training manuals and began exploring the beckoning field of solid-state electronics. He built various transistor circuits by scalping radios and junkyard TVs.

When he was 15, Steven secretly dissected his first padlock with his foster-father's grinder by removing the heads of the lock's rivets. At 17, he was making his own lockpicks and was considered a master lockpicker. He was "popping" Master combination padlocks by freehand manipulation and could open a Russwin six-spooled pin tumbler bank door lock with a safety pin and screwdriver. At age 18 he invented the magnetic padlock, which is still on the market today. That year he also enlisted in the U.S. Navy as an Aviation Electronics Technician. He was in boot camp when men landed on the moon.

He returned to civilian life with an honorable discharge in 1972 and then worked for a small telephone company as a switchman. While working there, he furthered his education with night school in the expanding field of digital electronics. (Since then he has worked as a machinist, a robotics technician, a computer lab technician, a machine maintenance technician, a locksmith, television repairman, and as an engineering technician, where he helped design and build cutting-edge robotics equipment.)

In 1974, Steven fell intoxicated with comparative religion and studied Eastern and Western philosophy from a score of noted and respected teachers. He became a practicing Buddhist in 1976. In 1979 he began three years of studying Tibetan White Crane Kung Fu under grand master Lucjan Shila. He spent two years studying jujitsu and wing chung under Sensei John Angelos.

By 1989, Steven had become intrigued with classical physics, primarily because of an anomaly known as the "Dean Drive." Invented in the late 1940s, these machines with "built-in wings" propel themselves using the centrifugal force of spinning weights. Such drives break three known laws of physics. Being the rebel that he is, Steven took on the task of rediscovering the long-lost secrets of the Dean Drive, which died with the well-known but controversial inventor Norman L. Dean in 1967.

Steven is also the author of a book on physics, *The Principles of Inertial Drive*. He has built several electric benchtop "inertial propulsion" drives, in which one engine pulls twice its weight, another smaller drive pulls three times its weight, while another machine displaces and holds its position while hanging from a stable, four-line ballistic pendulum. A larger, two-cycle, 37-pound engine loses more than half its weight while running—all from the force of elliptically orbiting rotors. (Inertial propulsion video will be available in July 2002 from <www.patentsecrets.com>.)